Creating Jobs
in the
21st Century

2ND EDITION

A NEW GLOBAL ECONOMIC DEVELOPMENT PARADIGM

ISBN: 1467920118

ISBN-13: 9781467920117

Published by: FINANCIAL PUBLISHING

Design by Don Gerron

Printed in the United States

This is an economic development plan for increasing global employment
by expanding the global home building industry
and increasing the demand for consumer products.

Additional information:

buildglobal.org

3219 E. Camelback # 421

Phoenix, Arizona 85018

DEDICATION

This book is dedicated to over four billion people on this planet that are struggling to stay alive on less than $2.50 US per day.

David R. Johns
June 16, 2012
buildglobal.org

CONTENTS

PART I: GLOBAL PROSPERTY
Build Global
A New Economic Development Paradigm 3
Demand for Consumer Goods 10

PART II: A GLOBAL ECONOMIC CRISIS
Global Unemployment. 19
Two Crisis 20
The Solution 20
Ending the Debate 21
Aggregate Demand by the People 22
Hayek or Keynesian 22
Who Is Advocating Keynesian and Why 24
John Maynard Keynes Fundamental Error 25
Friedrich A. Hayek Proven Correct. 27
Owning Appreciating Assets. 28
Economic Colonialism 30
Participatory Democracy 32
Deflecting Responsibility 33
A Point of Clarification 34

PART III: TIME FOR LEADERSHIP
Time for Action - Who Will Lead 41
Home Building Economics. 43
Lack of Leadership - Economic Turmoil 45
Immigration and Exporting Jobs. 47
Efforts to Reduce Immigration. 48
Close of an Era 50
The High Cost of Unemployment Benefits. 51
Food Stamps - Government Programs 51
Social Security in United States 52
Higher Revenue Required to Service Debt 53
Globalization 55
Trade Deficit 56
The Compounding Of the Problem 57
"No Thanks, I Got One" 57
A More Humane Solution 59

PART IV: POVERTY, THE OTHER CRISIS

Obedience to the Rules of Prosperity. 65
Economic Disparity between Nations 66
A Stalling Global Economy 69
Four Billion Living in Poverty 70
Three Billion More People By 2050 72
El Salvador Setting the Example 72
Home Building in Mexico. 73
Latin America Housing Financing Summit 74
How Many Homes Are Needed Globally. 74

PART V: PRINCIPLES OF PROSPERITY

New Product Consumers. 81
How to Create Jobs for the Unemployed 81
The Solution 82
Understanding Economics 83
Twelve Principles That Create People 84
How Do Developed Countries Benefit 94
Homebuilding Impacts Related Economies 95
Who Will Adopt Private Property Rights 97
Can Corruption be Eliminated 98
What Countries Will Participate. 100
How is Inflation Managed 101

PART VI: SUSTAINING EMPLOYMENT IN THE FUTURE

The Need is For More Product Consumers 107
Economic Freedom Creates Jobs 107
Seven Billion New Product Consumers. 108
Seven Billion New Taxpayers. 110
Free Trade Becomes Viable. 111
A Global Priority 113

PART VII: PARTICIPATORY ECONOMICS

A New Global Economic Paradigm 119
The King Bestowed the Private Rights 121
Independence 123
From Keynesian to Hayek Economics 124
Creating Prosperous Governments 127
Immigrants Succeed In Free Countries 128
Government Services. 130
Domestic Consumption 130

Buying and Selling Homes. 131
A Homebuilding Economy. 132
Attributes of a Construction Economy 133
Home Ownership Changes Cultural Beliefs 136

PART VIII: EMPIRICAL ECONOMIC DATA
Housing an Economic Indicator 143
Prosperity in United States of America. 144
Participatory Economics at the Start 145
Need For Five Million Homes in 1945. 147
Levittown Started The Housing Industry 147
Removal of Barriers to Prosperity 149
Protected Private Property Rights 150
Increasing Net Worth 151
Owning Property Is Not Unique to United States 156
Trade Creates Jobs Not Prosperous Nations 156

PART IX: MORTGAGE INSURANCE
Insured Mortgages 167
Financial Incentives 167
Guaranteed Title of Ownership Rights. 170
International Mortgage Insurance 170
Reinsuring Mortgages 171
International Agreements 172
Establishing a Process 181

PART X: ECONOMIC TRENDS
Economic Trends. 187
Excessive Personal Debt - Lowers Demand 188
Gross Domestic Product - United States 189
Increasing Labor Cost 190
China's Job Loss 191
Manufacturing Jobs Are Not A Solution 192
Small Handicraft Loans-Are Not A Solution 193
Domestic Buyers of Consumer Products 193
Domestic Investors. 196

PART XI: DESIGNING COMMUNITIES
New Villages for New Homes 203
Cost of Living 204
Social Cohesion 204

A New Urban Design 205
Natural Resources 206

EPILOGUE. 209
We Know Now

FIRST ADDENDUM: 217
Declaration of Independence

SECOND ADDENDUM: 221
Twelve Principles That Create Prosperous People

THIRD ADDENDUM: 231
What Can You Do

GLOSSARY: 239
A Global Vocabulary

BIBLIOGRAPHY 245

PART I
GLOBAL PROSPERITY

GLOBAL PROSPERITY

Enormous opportunities for businesses in America and Globally are established by expanding the global home building industry in emerging economies. The adoption of the Build Global economic development paradigm energizes the American and Global economies to an unprecedented level creating literally hundreds of millions of new jobs worldwide. Creating Jobs in the 21st Century explains why establishing a new economic development paradigm that calls for the construction of millions of homes in emerging economies is the only strategy that will actually increase global employment and prosperity for all people.

Increasing employment in the emerging economies will reverse the flow of legal and illegal immigration. Creating Jobs in the 21st Century is a humane and viable solution to the global economic crisis. Building homes begins the process of eradicating severe global poverty, reducing economic disparity globally, and increasing international trade.

This new economic development paradigm calls for trillions of dollars to be invested in banks in emerging economies. The local banks in turn invest in *first mortgages loans to millions of existing, qualifying borrowers* in those countries that have adopted private property rights. The paradigm creates jobs in all sectors of the global economy by funding home loans that in turn always creates an enormous demand for consumer goods. This approach to funding aid requires the restructure of the each emerging economy in a manner according to the Twelve Principles That Create Prosperous People which enables the people to go to work and help themselves by insuring their natural right; the opportunity of investing in their local economy.

"BUILD GLOBAL"
A NEW ECONOMIC
DEVELOPMENT PARADIGM

The viability of this home building paradigm has been proven by the incredible increase in prosperity in the United States of America that has been achieved in just sixty years utilizing the same paradigm. Eradicating extreme global poverty is limited only by the degree of responsiveness from the global political and financial leaders that have the power and financial capability for implementing this plan.

It is imperative that the world understand how the changes that have occurred in the needs and demands for consumer goods have rendered the old global economic paradigm obsolete. The evidence of a deteriorating global economy proves that the economic structure of the old paradigm no longer has the ability to manufacture and exchange consumer goods in a manner that creates jobs.

The concept of improving our technology and creating new products that can be exported will not restore our economy. Proposing such a solution demonstrates a complete lack of understanding of the basic economics that created this country. It also illustrates an ignorance of the changes in the demographics of the more industrialized nations and how the changes have decreased demand for manufactured goods. Most consumers already have all of the consumer products they need.

The economy of the United States is not just experiencing another cyclical recession or depression. The economy is experiencing a global

economic crisis because the needs and demands of the emerging affluent generations have diminished.

What we need are hundreds of millions of new jobs that will produce hundreds of millions of new product consumers. Product consumers with buying power will restore manufacturing employment
globally. The crisis can only be solved with adoption of a new global
economic development plan that shifts the home building industry
that has been the driving force in the American and Global economy
for sixty years to the emerging economies that need millions of jobs
and houses.

It has become painfully obvious that the leadership in the United
States has no understanding of what is happening to our economy and
do not have any ideas as to how to increase employment in America.

Uninformed attempts by the "Amateur" to sustain the people and create employment have increased the federal debt to over
$15,673,229,783, 378 as of May 2012. Amateur, is a new book by
Edward Klein, explaining why our president has failed horribly with
his "tax and spend" idea of a solution to the unemployment problem.
It should be required reading for all Americans concerned about the
future of America.

The economic crisis is being brought on, partially, by the changing birth rates in the United States and Western Europe. With a
declining birth rate it is not possible for the United States to experience a housing boom that would employ millions workers in the near
future. The projected lack of demand for housing is a result of population trends that are already established by the diminishing birth rate.

What is happening to the global work force is perfectly described
in "The Coming Generational Storm" a book by Laurence J. Kotlikoff
and Scot Burns. They explain in increase in the medium age impacts
our future prosperity. A true understanding of what has happened
must become the basis of any new attempts to raise the employment
level in American and Western European economies if we are to save
the global economy. The following birth rate statistics seem to vary

on the internet, but these approximations will serve the purpose of illustrating the four "housing booms" we have experienced to date.

The housing demand and the economy in the United States have been directly related to the population boom and home construction cycles that began with the birth of the Baby Boomers.

Baby Boomers were born during the period of 1946-1964. They came of age as major consumers in the period 1964-1982. Their total population has been estimated at seventy-eight million.

Generation X followed. They were born in the period of 1965-1981, and came of age in 1983-1999. They totaled fifty-one million.

Generation Y, the third generation, known as the Millennial Generation were born in the period 1982-2001. They come of age in 2000-2018. Totaling seventy-five million they were a major influence on housing construction during 2000-2008. The supply actually exceeded the demands, which means that we have adequate housing to meet current demands.

Generation Z, the fourth generation being born during the period of 2002-2020 will not start coming of age as major consumers for eight more years in 2020-2038. However it appears that the total population of Generation Z will, based on actual birth statistics, be approximately twenty-three million. The current birth rate is less than 2.1 per woman. If it continues at the current rate over the next ten years, it will not create a housing boom when they start to come of age.

As can be seen the low rate of increase in our population cannot possibly create the demand for housing that has energized our economy in the past. When we consider that there is an oversupply of housing on the market, the probability of another housing boom in the next thirty to forty years is simply not possible.

It is also very important to recognize that the first of the Baby Boomer Generation reached sixty years of age in 2006. As they go into homes for elderly and die over the next ten to fifteen years, millions of their homes will be coming onto the market.

This is compounded by the fact that the birth rate for Generation Z has fallen below the reproduction rate required to maintain a stable population. To reach the former level of increases in population that created housing booms Generation Z would have to more than double the current birth rate. Assuming that Generation Z consist of approximately ten million women to reach the level of population that created home building booms in the past they would have to an average of seven children to reach seventy million population boom. This means that the next generation will not support the current level of manufacturing capacity that was built on demands of fifty million to seventy millions people.

The birth rate in most countries in the European Union is also below the reproduction rate required to maintain a stable population. This is creating unemployment in the EU and economic decline also because of the decline in the global demand for consumer products.

As a result of this in birth rate decline, the demand by current consumers in the more industrialized countries will no longer be sufficient to support past levels of employment in all sectors. The solution to this global economic crisis is to increase employment in emerging economies. An increase in global employment will increase demands for consumer products worldwide and energize global manufacturing.

Each downturn in employment in United States is due to a slowdown in home construction, followed by layoffs in manufacturing and a reduction in trade brought about by the buildup of supply exceeding demand.

In this recent cycle, the global manufacturing production capability increased rapidly to meet unusually high consumer demands. When it was operating at full capacity, it fulfilled orders quickly and exceeded global demands for consumer products by the much slower emerging population of consumers. This resulted in a major reduction in the number of employees needed during a normal production cycle. At the same time, the number of migrant workers available in the more industrialized countries was increasing.

Consumers have reached a saturation point. Sales are down and consumer confidence is at an extreme low. Major retailers are closing stores. Without a significant increase in consumer demand, there will be insufficient support to achieve the former high levels of employment. Unemployment will continue to rise.

After World War II when global trade began to expand for the first time, the global economy revolved around the consumer demands of the faster industrializing economies. Over the years when the United States was experiencing a healthy housing boom, imports were up. The economies of other countries were also energized as manufacturing employment expanded to meet the export demand. The global economic trends were a function of the cycles of the more industrialized economies and their demand for imported products. The economies of Japan, Korea, and China were energized to the point that they became capable of expanding their economies and took over a major portion of the global manufacturing. Manufacturing employment fell by sixty percent in many of the more industrialized economies. The resulting unemployment, when added to the large number of legal and illegal workers that immigrated to the United States and Europe has created a financial burden for the people and their governments which is increasing this economic crisis.

Because there are too many people and too few jobs, there is a reduction in the demand for consumer goods both domestic and imported. It is imperative to increase the demand for consumer goods to a level that will increase global employment. To do this, there must be more consumers. Where can we find four billion new consumers? They are four billion people living on less than $2.50 per day waiting for the opportunity to be employed and become product consumers. The financing of homes creates jobs. Jobs create product consumers.

The ownership and sale of homes is the one economic process that builds personal wealth among the lower income groups because their rent payments are converted to principle payments and the reduction of debt on an appreciating asset.

Very few business or political leaders appreciate the fact that the availability of insured mortgages started a process that raised the standard of living for hundreds of millions of Americans in only sixty years.

The idea that people must own assets that appreciate in value over time in order to build a prosperous national economy is not included in our economic text books. This is the most important principle that must be adhered to when changing the economy of any nation striving to seriously increase the prosperity of its people. Building homes increases demand for consumer goods by the people on a very large scale. This, of course, is what determines the level of manufacturing employment.

Once this proposal is understood by men and women everywhere, many experienced in business, title management, law, real estate development, construction, and mortgage financing will want to become involved in addressing the global employment issue. They will want to help to expand the international home financing program for emerging economies by moving to the countries with protected, private property rights. Many of those that have immigrated to the USA and Western Europe to find work are now experienced in real estate development and construction. They will want to return to their native land where the opportunities to help eradicate poverty will be enormous.

As the new economic development paradigm and the homebuilding industry become a reality it will reverse the direction of the current immigration trends. Building up the economies of the emerging nations is the correct way to help people in need and is a more humane approach to helping those who are struggling support their families. This plan is a viable solution to global unemployment. There is no excuse for delaying the acceleration of our efforts to reduce global poverty and homelessness while creating jobs globally and strengthening the global economy.

There is nothing more important to billions of people that are suffering from unemployment than solving the problem that has created the unemployment crisis.

We are experiencing a new type of economic disruption in global economy. Solving the problem requires a new method of creating the aggregate demand and production of consumer goods. We must stop ignoring over four billion people on the planet that need our help. It is our ethical responsibility to help them find work and purchase their basic needs.

We must work together to finance the development of emerging economies and begin the establishment of universal prosperity. The emerging prosperity will reduce the extreme economic disparity between nations that limits the economic development of all nations.

Once people everywhere begin to understand the power of this proposal they will agree that it is time for Americans to join with others internationally to take the lead in calling attention to the needs of billions of people who are suffering because of the lack of jobs.

The adoption of this proposal to develop an international economic development plan should become the first priority of every nation and its people who are interested in increasing aggregate demand and employment worldwide.

Implementing this proven strategy is unquestionably a global imperative. The American economy and the global economy are now irrevocably linked to the development of housing globally because the old economic development paradigm is dead.

Bernard Baumohl author of *The Secrets of Economic Indicators*[1] points this out but also identifies what could be viewed as an exception.

Baumohl writes:

> "Looking for a single infallible indicator that can foresee the future direction of the economy? Forget it: you won't find any. However, there is one that comes surprisingly close, and that is housing. Excluding one instance, there has never been a recession in the U.S. at a time when the housing sector stood strong.

Only once since the end of World War II did the economy contract despite a robust housing market, and that was in 2001. Even then, the recession was brief and not very deep. This impressive track record is why many experts view home building as one of the most reliable leading indicators of economic activity."

It is also the main source of funding for sound economic activity. It is the transferring of the United State methodology for creating prosperity based on building homes for those who qualify to the emerging economies that will increase global demand for consumer products.

Increasing demand for consumer products is the only method of economic development that is a reliable process that increases manufacturing and retail employment.

DEMAND FOR CONSUMER PRODUCTS

Simply put, the proposal is to adopt the exact process for emerging economies that has been the used in the United States to create prosperity for sixty years. In the United States, financing is provided for construction of homes at all price levels for those who are employed and affluent and qualify for a standard home loan. This is a process that has created millions of jobs that have resulted in enormous increases in demands for consumer goods and manufacturing jobs.

Building homes in entirely new planned communities that are completely serviced with retail and office development in each emerging economy will be the solution for those seeking better housing now.

Trillions of dollars will be required to construct the hundreds of millions of home that are currently needed worldwide. The plan calls for the international banking community to make conventional loans through the domestic banks in emerging countries. Home loans will increase global employment for many years and will prevent the pending global economic crisis while accelerating the eradication of severe poverty.

The expansion of the global home building industry to include emerging economies solves two crises, global unemployment and global poverty.

The plan is based on an investment program that would concentrate on financing and developing housing projects for only those that qualify for a standard home loan initially. The newly employed will also become qualified as construction begins. (See the ***Twelve Principles that Create Prosperous People*** in Chapter Four.)

If you are concerned about global unemployment and the extreme poverty consuming the lives of billions of people, read and study this plan. Determine how you can join others in this effort in your own country and internationally. A new international economic paradigm cannot be established without an international effort and a new international economic development covenant between nations. The need is to create twice as many jobs as now exist.

This plan describes how it is now possible in the 21st century to launch a viable economic solution to global poverty and provide international employment. The demand for jobs, based on the current projections of population, will require an increase in employment that is at least twice the number currently employed. It is a plan by which a global economic crisis can be averted while eradicating severe poverty.

Universal prosperity can be accomplished in emerging economies because of several global economic conditions that are conductive to financing home building are already present in the global economies at this time.

Extremely large capital reserves are languishing for lack of investment opportunities. The slow economy is resulting in few investment opportunities. The slow economy is resulting in few expanding businesses. Should those holding the languishing capital decide to invest trillions of dollars in mortgages in emerging economies, it would launch a major expansion of all types of new business opportunities worldwide.

There are many partially free and free nations seeking financial assistance in their struggle to change laws, provide housing, and eradicate poverty. As people gain freedom, and are able to establish private property rights viable financing of businesses and homes in developing countries is already becoming a reality.

Millions of qualified workers are available globally to begin development and construction. Many of those that have migrated to the more industrialized economies have become educated and trained. They are available to return to their native land as part of the management and training of the work force that will be needed for the development of housing. Many now own their own business and will have the opportunity to start another as part of the enormous demand for experienced people.

There are millions of prospective borrowers that are working and affluent. They will qualify for a mortgage to purchase a modern new home. The net worth of the upper 20% of the population in emerging countries is in the trillions of dollars.

Once private property rights are established, those in the emerging economies will have an opportunity to purchase a new modern, fully developed home in a new community with schools, retail stores and commercial services.

The transition will be a major upgrade in quality and a viable investment for the new home owners. This proposal describes a few basic terms that are used in the real estate development process. It briefly describes technical disciplines that govern the business of real estate for those who may not have experience in the field or have never participated in an economy based on home ownership.

A short glossary of real estate terms to be used in the development process is provided to ensure a clear understanding by participants. The plan explains to those that have worked in a homebuilding industry what might be taught to others around the world about real estate development and home construction in an effort to build a common vocabulary.

This plan is for the establishment of a paradigm shift in the entire global economic structure. It interjects enormous amounts of capital into emerging economies through the hands of the working people.

The construction of homes will create employment in the countries that cannot be established by any other method. The newly employed will be able to purchase their basic needs and a home for themselves. As they pay off their home mortgage the home owners will experience an increase in their net worth.

The needs of an entire economy are met under this type of financing. Governments taxing the process will collect development fees and tax revenues on each of the mortgage disbursements. The amount collected by governments will eventually equal the total amount of all of the principle of all mortgages that are funded as the funds move through the economies and are taxed on each turn over.

The government receives tax revenues from an expanding economy to service the debt on money borrowed and used for the construction of the many services needed throughout each emerging nation. When governments finance improvements with borrowed funds, they take on debt. History has shown that when lending to governments for capital improvements which do not improve the economy sufficiently to increase tax revenues to repay the debt there can be a regional economic crisis.

It is the credit of people that qualify for a home loan that finances the increase in national prosperity. The economy is actually the result of funds being disbursed from the debt incurred by all of the home owners.

PART II

A GLOBAL ECONOMIC CRISIS

Creating an enormous increase in aggregate demand for consumer products will stimulate global employment now and in future years. It must become the number one global priority. The adoption of this plan for Creating Jobs in the 21st Century will result in a major increase in global employment. It will revive global economies. It will increase employment in both the more industrialized countries and emerging economies by creating millions of new consumers making demands for consumer products.

GLOBAL UNEMPLOYMENT

The plan is directed to those of you living in more industrialized countries, searching for a solution to unemployment problems threatening the stability of the global economy. This plan is also addressed to you who are living in countries struggling to increase employment, provide housing, and eradicate poverty but are unaware of the twelve principles that create prosperity.

This plan overcomes the two major problems that have restricted the development of emerging economies in the past. The strategy is based on the international banking community lending money directly to domestic banks in emerging economies for the purpose of making home loans. This approach is based on the Friedrich A. Hayek approach to creating aggregate demand. It is an approach to increasing prosperity that places the people at the center of the earning and disbursing of money used in financing the economy of a nation.

Past attempts have failed in their attempts to fund governments and corporations for the creation of jobs in emerging economies as well as more industrialized economies. This plan increases global employment by selecting and implementing proven economic principles to achieve universal prosperity.

Under this plan it is necessary to establish protected, private property rights in emerging economies. The leadership of the emerging economies must come to understand that mortgage funds will both energize the economy as well as finance government investments in schools, medical facilities, and infrastructure through taxation of the process once private property laws permit mortgage financing. (See the First Addendum: The Declaration of Independence.)

TWO CRISES

There are actually two crucial global unemployment crises. Both crises must be resolved before a major recovery in the global economy can become a reality. The first crisis is the slowdown in manufacturing due to the lack of aggregate demand for consumer products. The second crisis is the humiliating and reprehensible increase in the degree of global poverty in emerging economies.

The increase in global poverty has been ignored. Americans in the United States struggle with obesity while people in many countries continue to starve. Their cry for help is not even mentioned on the nightly news. No one has thought of a viable economic program that the more industrialized nations could establish to eradicate poverty and create prosperous nations. Unemployment in these struggling economies and its associated poverty are not being discussed. The more than four billion people starving, struggling to live under inconceivably cruel conditions in the 21st Century need our attention.

These two seemingly unrelated crises have now become interrelated as part of the growing economic disaster. The resolution of each has become dependent on the resolution of the other. What is creating the unemployment crisis and why could the problems turn our global economy into a global calamity? In identifying the cause of the economic problems it becomes clear why the proposed strategy will reenergize the global economy. With the adoption of this strategy, the two crises are solved as one problem.

WHAT IS THE SOLUTION

Industrialized countries are experiencing major economic problems because of lack of demand for their products. They are failing in their efforts to create jobs because elected officials do not know what is creating the unemployment. To increase demand for consumer products, there must be an increase in employment. Consumers must have the funds to purchase goods.

As this economic depression began to develop and tax revenues declined, the borrowing and spending of many nations and states increased to finance unrealistic budgets. This is now bringing governments around the world to the edge of a major economic disaster. Elected officials are relying on government programs to energize the economies, hoping the programs will cause a recovery in its normal cycle as occurred in the past. *These attempts are being made without understanding the evolving changes in the needs of the public and how these changes have destroyed the old global paradigm for doing business.*

The economies of millions of people around the world are linked to the purchase of imports by the people of the United States, Europe and other industrialized nations. Their prosperity has become very interdependent with the prosperity of the more industrialized nations as a result of increased trade. However, demands of consumers in these economies have changed. This is forcing a new global economic structure to emerge, based on understanding the needs of the people in emerging economies. A plan must be adopted that will meet the needs of both industrialized nations and emerging economies. Under the terms of this plan it is possible to prepare a detailed program to increase trade in both directions and restore the global economy.

ENDING THE DEBATE

To develop trade and increase global prosperity it is necessary to understand that there are two fundamental economic theories about creating prosperous economies that have been debated and tried for over seventy years. One is based on the principles of capitalism. These principles guide a free market economy and function according to the economics of supply and demand.

The other is based on the theory that an economy must be managed by a central government that intervenes in our business efforts in an attempt to create prosperity by increasing aggregate demand by government taxing, spending, and manipulation of interest rates. The later theory attempts to influence an economy by taxing the people and spending the money on government programs or buying an ownership in businesses. Government ownership of businesses does not increase aggregate demand. It destroys free economies.

None of these government intervention ideas are based on experience and reality. We are experiencing the fact that economic recessions become depressions when these theories are applied to the economy.

AGGREGATE DEMAND BY THE PEOPLE

The adoption of twelve correct principles for use in the establishment of an economy increases aggregate demand for goods and services. It enables the people to earn more money and spend it on consumer goods, new businesses, and employment of others which creates more jobs and increases the prosperity of a nation. (See the Second Addendum).

HAYEK OR KEYNESIAN

A viable approach for creating aggregate demand was advanced by Friedrich A. Hayek, an Austrian economist in the 1930s. He taught in England and the United States, eventually becoming a British citizen. As his teachings were applied, they became the basis of the capitalistic approach to creating employment and were proven to be very successful in the creation of national prosperity in United States. Hayek understood that the only way to increase aggregate demand was to enable people to increase the amount of money they could earn and spend for their own needs and desires.

He taught that private property ownership was the only method by which people could increase the amount they earned above the typical labor rate. Private property provides the means for private production.

It creates self-employment as well as employment for others. This leads naturally to a demand for and creation of more goods and services.

Hayek wrote *The Road to Serfdom* in 1944 and renewed the book in 1972.

> "What our generation has forgotten is that the system of private property is the most important guaranty of freedom, not only for those who own property, but scarcely less for those that do not. It is only because the control of the means of production is divided among many people acting independently, that nobody has complete power over us, that we as individuals can decide what to do with ourselves. If all the means of production were vested in a single hand, whether it be nominally that of "society" as a whole or that of a dictator, whoever exercises this control has complete power over us."

> Hayek taught that it is our individual efforts acting in our own behalf that creates the means of production and the demand for consumer goods. This maintains our personal freedom. His teachings in economics are in direct opposition to the theories of John Maynard Keynes being advanced in Washington, DC by President Obama and his team. For people who do not have a concept of how the economy actually functions, it is difficult to come up with new ideas for energizing the economy.

However, that is not an excuse for resurrecting the failed economic theories of Keynes in an attempt to energize the United States economy and create employment.

Their approach demonstrates a complete lack of knowledge of how many times this has been tried by many countries. Germany tried the Keynes approach and wisely switched almost immediately.

Greece, France and other members of the EU have tried Keynesian Economics in recent years and have been forced into major economic problems.

What Dick Morris and Eileen McGann predicted in their 2009 publication of *CATASTROPHE...AND HOW TO FIGHT BACK,*[iii] has now occurred. They wrote.

"President Obama pledges to bring us back to prosperity, to end the recession. But his polices are likely to do the opposite—casting us into a full-scale, long-lasting depression. At the very least, his huge spending will bring inflation and even more economic pain. And in many ways, Obama's program undermines the very business confidence that will be essential to restoring normal economic activity. We are hostage to an ideologue who wants to use this crisis – not solve it –to promote his dogmatic agenda."

WHO IS ADVOCATING KEYNESIAN ECONOMICS AND WHY

The debate on how to increase aggregate demand has been going on for over seventy years. Increasing aggregate demand by the people increases employment. Housing construction increases employment and consumer demand which increases manufacturing employment.

Many policymakers and economists in the United States and countries around the world still believe in the theories of British economist John Maynard Keynes expressed in his book, *The General Theory of Employment, Interest and Money.*[iv]

Keynes is credited with saying that economic downturns are explained by a lack of insufficient aggregate demand, and that government policies have the ability to stimulate aggregate demand and improve prosperity. He believed government should become involved in the process of doing business when there is a fear that the economy may go into a recession or depression. He proposed the theory that governments should take over and own or regulate businesses, spend tax revenue on government projects and manipulate interest rates in an attempt to increase aggregate demand for consumer products.

He believed that governments should be free to also increase individual taxes and spend the money on government programs. He did not delineate what type of demand could be created by government spending or how it would develop the economy. Each time his theories have been put into practice, the borrowing and spending by governments accelerated the process that was creating a depression. In Europe there is still evidence of what this approach to economics will do to the people. His plan is now known as Keynesian Theory of Economics. His theories were not founded on the understanding of the Twelve Principles of Participatory Economics, which allows people to borrow and invest in the economy of their country when they possess the right to own private property.

KEYNES'S FUNDAMENTAL ERROR

The writings of Keynes did not consider ownership of private property and its key contribution to increased prosperity. This is the fundamental error in his theories.

For example, the aggregate demand for manufactured products by Americans in the United States was increased when 1,850,000 families borrowed an average of $250,000 each to pay for the construction of a home in one year, as they did in the U.S. in 2005.

Introducing $462 billion into the economy in a twelve-month period not only created aggregate demand, it produced the type of jobs that are the stabilizing force of the economy if not interrupted by the careless intervention by legislators.

People raise their standard of living as this process is repeated year after year. It is an annual process based on demand and supply in nations that guarantee and protect the right of individuals to buy and own private property.

Keynes taught that in cases where monetary policies are ineffective, governments can rely on fiscal policies such as increasing spending by borrowing. However, the increase in interest cost from borrowing creates an increase in taxes. This reduces the ability of the people to finance businesses or start new businesses which are required for reducing unemployment. The government borrowing to support an economy will not energize an economy. The government debt payments created by failed government programs will continue to reduce the ability of the people to prosper for years.

There are fewer funds available for consumer products after paying higher taxes to pay the interest on the increase in debt. It will also reduce the imports which impacts the global economy as well.

Redirecting the national economy must be addressed as a global problem impacting the prosperity of all men and women on our interdependent planet.

As leaders around the world search for a solution to their domestic economic predicament, new programs are still being introduced in an effort to create new jobs.

Decision makers are wrong when characterizing their economic turmoil as a domestic problem while ignoring how their economy has been impacted by the international economic crisis. Without considering the true nature of the evolving interdependent economies, their attempts are resulting in failure.

These leaders do not understand current trends in global economics. It is no longer possible for nations to solve what they perceive as domestic economic problems with legislation that does not recognize the changes in the needs of all people.

The reduction in the needs of affluent consumers is establishing a new worldwide economic structure in the 21st century. This redefines how manufacturing capacities will expand in the future. Past experiments in funding international corporations and governments in underdeveloped nations have proven that it is a failed strategy. It will not create sufficient well-paying jobs that increase demand for their consumer products domestically in order to energize the economy.

In a book entitled *The Global Economic Crisis*[v] edited by Michel Chossudovsky and Andrew Gavin Marshall, Chossudovsky wrote:

"....the macroeconomic policy agenda of the Obama administration does not constitute a solution to the crisis.

In fact, quite the opposite: it directly contributes to the concentration and centralization of financial wealth, which in turn undermines the real economy."

HAYEK PROVEN CORRECT

Unfortunately, the Hayek principle was not put into practice during the late 1930s when Franklin D. Roosevelt, President of the United States, was following the theories of John Maynard Keynes. He was spending money on government projects.

The people in United States and other countries around the world suffered from the lack of employment because they were also trying Keynesian theories.

People had barely enough for daily substance; many formed bread lines. They had no discretionary income to spend on consumer goods and services which limited the growth of manufacturing and service employment. Under the Keynesian economic theories, a socialist type government that taxed and spent evolved in many nations. The global economy was in an unemployment crisis similar to the present one for the same reasons.

With the establishment of insured home mortgages in the United States, Mr. Hayek was proven to have the correct approach to creating prosperity after World War II ended. Millions of people were able to borrow large amounts of money that was to be paid back over thirty years. They spent the funds in one year for a home.

This infusion of capital through the hands of the people created aggregate demand because they held private property rights. This fuelled the economy. This is exactly what Hayek had proposed.

Some years later President Ronald Reagan of the United States and Prime Minister Margaret Thatcher of England, both believers in principles defined by Hayek, were able to turn around their national economies by their application of Hayek Economics.

The production of homes over the past sixty years has not only increased aggregate demand according to the economic principles of Hayek, it has stabilized the economy when there has been little or no government interference. The economy of the United States of America has not experienced uncontrollable inflation because the basic twelve principles are in effect.

OWNING APPRECIATING ASSETS

To overcome the lack of economic development of any nation, it is necessary to understand and address how investments and financing must be made through the hands of the people by funding home construction and small business loans and triggered the expansion of the manufacturing capacity in the United States. (See the Third Addendum.)

An expanding manufacturing capacity cannot be sustained merely by the minimal demands of workers employed at minimal wages. There simply is not enough demand created by limited discretionary income from those drawing low wages and the rollover of their funds disbursed from ordinary income.

There are over 120 million modern homes in America today for a population of just over three hundred million. The economic development plan proposed for increasing aggregate demand on a global scale is patterned after this same proven plan. Simply put, the people, given the financial tools such as borrowing and investing, become the driving force that creates a prosperous domestic economy. It is their willingness to take on debt that established the American prosperity.

It is clearly understood that for many years, in many countries struggling with poverty and homelessness, there was a cultural stigma placed on those that borrowed money for any purpose.

It was believed that each person should manage their affairs within their own means. Unfortunately, this has not worked out for the betterment of the people. The attitude denied people the freedom to act and become part of the investment community. It did not recognize the economic principle that requires people borrow and spend according to their ability to repay the loan. This is the economic principle that energizes an economy.

Nobel Prize-winning economist Milton Friedman said:

"I think that nothing is as important for freedom as recognizing in the law each individual's natural right to property, and giving individuals a sense that they own something that they are responsible for, that they have control over, and that they can dispose of." (Interview with Hillsdale College President Larry Arnn, May 22, 2006)

Friedman could have also said that the right to own private property is critically important for the establishment of a prosperous economy.

A legal system that grants and protects the right to own property, combined with the right and opportunity to borrow money in order to buy a home is the basis for prosperity. It involves people in the economic development process in a manner that allows them to own an appreciating asset that creates wealth over time. They could not accomplish this in any other way while only working for wages.

International financing of home construction in emerging economies will level the global playing field by creating jobs and reducing economic disparity. The resulting domestic prosperity will reduce and, in time, eliminate the current dependence on exports. Exports tend to go down and become a much smaller part of the economy while imports go up as homes are being constructed. At the same time, trade can increase because of the reduction in economic disparity between nations due to the increase in jobs and prosperity.

Empirical evidence of this is seen in statistics of the United States economy. The United States has succeeded in the past economically, not because of how much they sell to other countries (the U.S. infamously buys twice as much as it sells in the international marketplace), but because of how much they produce and sell within their own borders.

Americans prior to the recent down turn could afford to buy what they produce, while workers in poor countries cannot afford to purchase more than a subsistence amount of the goods they produce and the crops they grow.

The United States and other nations with healthy home building industries have succeeded because they increased the prosperity of their people, and have been self-sustaining based on domestic demands.

Government agencies and institutions become more viable because the same economic foundation which keeps the private sector vibrant also generates tax revenues at all levels of government, which in turn provides the financial resources to deliver the services people need such as hospitals, schools, and infrastructure.

ECONOMIC COLONIALISM

The globalization process that confines people to minimum wage jobs in emerging economies is, to put it bluntly, economic colonialism. By not permitting and enforcing private property rights, people become economic dependents of a system of governance, both domestic and foreign, that is as unjust and uncivilized as slave ownership.

The involvement of all men and women in emerging economies is necessary if we are to succeed in improving the global economy. We must improve personal freedom as well as economic and physical well-being.

Because of economic colonialism, the degree of poverty has increased to such a level that we are now experiencing a global health emergency. Laurie Garret, author of ***Betrayal of Trust, The Collapse of Global Public Health***,[vi] explains that because of increasing poverty, tens of millions are dying of new, untreatable forms of tuberculosis, malaria, staph, and other organisms while millions more are dying of AIDS.

Yet current strategies have done little to change the limits to economic freedom that exists in some of the underdeveloped countries. People in these countries do not have the right or the means to be full participants in the economy.

Most are economic slaves bound to political systems that recognize few if any political or economic rights for the vast majority of their citizens. Millions of others are forced to illegally immigrate and enter into a different form of economic slavery, living in the shadows, in an attempt to reduce the poverty that grips their families at home.

When the political leadership of any nation becomes convinced it is best to adopt this economic plan for establishing economic freedom for all, it will create hundreds of millions of jobs for that nation.

It eliminates the need for people to leave their homelands and encourages those that have immigrated to return home. When a country decides to join the program and agrees to provide protected private property rights for all, the financing of home construction could be achieved on such a large scale that many that have immigrated in the search for jobs will return to their native land. The opportunities for employment and participation in the emerging economies will be enormous. Increased employment will allow the emerging economies to increase their demands for consumer products. This will increase employment globally.

In countries torn by internal strife, where people are seeking freedom from oppression, a home ownership program would provide a reason for the leaders to cooperate. It will allow the people to succeed rather than become involved with terrorists. When the people become employed, buy a home and begin to feel the effects of freedom and prosperity, terrorist will find little support for their brutal and barbaric dominance.

PARTICIPATORY DEMOCRACY

It is crucial to recognize that if the economic principles of prosperity are not the foundation of a nation's democratic process, participatory democracy is a facade and its men and women remain in circumstances that are little more than economic serfdom.

Today as many as two billion people enjoy a level of prosperity that was unimaginable just sixty years ago. Some countries, notably the U.S., Canada, Germany, Japan and South Korea, have not only raised their standard of living substantially over the past fifty to sixty years, but many previously poor people in a number of developed nations have become incredibly wealthy.

The story is very different for billions of people in struggling countries where economic colonialism has been accepted. The vast majority of these people are industrious and many are educated, but they live in nations where the laws and the economic system deny them the path to prosperity by investing in their nation's economy. Unless they can find jobs, they are treated as mere tools of industry and government; economic slaves to systems governed by people who either prefer the poor to remain in economic captivity, or are totally ignorant of how nations can become prosperous, or perhaps both.

Reducing unemployment through what has been labeled Globalization is obviously not the answer. Employing hard working people in factories is not the answer. Billions of people in nations around the world work very hard at skilled jobs every day. In most countries, there are millions of employed teachers, police officers, health care providers, government workers, construction laborers, and skilled and semiskilled workers of all trades.

They are unable to do anything more than barely provide for their families while hoping and praying that inflation does not drive them further into poverty and despair.

Increasing the level of education by itself is not an answer, although it will be very important when this plan succeeds. Raising the level of education without a plan in countries where there are no expanding businesses has resulted in "Brain Drain."

The more intelligent and better educated must flee their native land to find jobs and then send money home to support their family. This decreases the effort to change the system because of the lack of leadership. This plan enables the educated and experienced to find jobs at home and work to create prosperity for all. This will help all people in these countries to reach their potential and become prosperous at home.

DEFLECTING RESPONSIBILITY

In places where people are struggling just to keep their families alive, hopelessness easily becomes epidemic. Many of these people have heard empty promises that factory employment (globalization) will improve their lot in life; that the prosperous nations of the world will help raise their standard of living. It has not happened and they fear it never will. In some countries, dictatorial rulers and other radicals deflect the people's discontent by blaming the world's prosperous nations for the people's poverty and hopelessness.

This stirs up anger and resentment that can be used by terrorists for manipulating the people to their evil purposes. For many of the world's desperately poor people, the terrorists call to arms strikes a resonant chord. The continuing behavior of some of the world's wealthy nations is held up to those that are suffering as evidence of the indifference to their plight. The more prosperous countries have been accused of imperialism.

The truth is that the poor and the starving have been prevented from participating in a prosperous world economy because of their economic systems. A nation without an economic development plan that includes private propter rights and home ownership for all the people prohibits economic growth for all.

When this effort to increase global prosperity is proven successful, it is highly probable that terrorist or ambitious tyrants will find it very difficult to find support. No one will want to become involved with any ambitious programs that could result in the loss of their hard earned prosperity. Each family will have something worth preserving for themselves and their children. The time has come to heal and forgive. It is time to us, the more prosperous, to help two billion people who have real problems. It is time to stop waging wars and killing people because they do not share your beliefs. In the Unites States, it is time to stop the bickering and fault finding. It is time to pull together and solve these two international crises simultaneously.

A POINT OF CLARIFICATION

The theories advanced by the world's economists often attempt to explain why the poor become poorer under some systems of governance, cultural belief, or geographic limitation.

Over years of research, I have found no mention in economic discussions and books of how mortgage financing has increased the prosperity in developed nations over the past fifty to sixty years.

Economists apparently have no knowledge of how loaning funds for home construction to individuals created aggregate demand for consumer products and services such as home building materials and consumer goods.

Most economists attribute increases in prosperity to the increase in the number of manufacturing jobs without any knowledge of how those jobs were launched by an increase in demand for consumer products. Working people create enormous aggregate demand by borrowing funds on appreciating assets. Few economists acknowledge any connection between one of the most prosperous economies in history and the phenomenon of widespread home ownership in United States.

Current theories fail to grasp the principles that permit people to participate in a plan which places them at the very center of economic development. Men and women use their credit and borrow capital to become investors in their own economy. This is the driving force of an expanding prosperity.

In recent years, political leaders in many countries have begun to take over ownership in businesses. Governments using the excuse that companies are struggling to make a profit, take over the business governments and fund their losses. The argument is that they are too big to be allowed to fail. This is propagandized as a solution to the lack of employment and the down turn in prosperity. In fact, it is an attempt to manipulate the people in a grab for power and money by the elite. This leads to centralizing power and destroying an economy.

Too often interference by governments in free enterprise has had disastrous results in countries that have tried them. Their attempts have also proven that the increase in the size of the government created is dangerous to the health and welfare of the people because of high taxes, enforcement power and limited freedom to act. Both Germany and England experimented with large centralized governments. They now are managed according to principles associated with capitalism.

The August 7, 2010 issue of *The Economist* magazine reported that, "Nine of the world's thirty largest listed firms are emerging market companies that count the state as their dominate shareholder." This cannot continue if the economy is to be free and open for new investment. The economic theories of Fredrick Hayek must become once again the only approach to creating prosperity for the United States and emerging economies.

It is time for a new global economic development plan based on tried and proven principles that can be adopted by emerging nations who are striving to eradicate poverty and homelessness.

PART III

A TIME FOR LEADERSHIP

Many people are talking about creating jobs while waiting for the economy to recover. Talk is cheap. This plan for investment promises enormous improvement in global employment in the near term. It will trigger other investments in preparation for a strong global economy. We need a leader who understands these new global economic needs and their interrelationship.

A TIME FOR ACTION - WHO WILL LEAD

There is no question that the United States must invest in upgrading educational programs, and research and development of new products, as well as reduce taxes on corporations as an incentive to encourage corporations to return their allegiance to the United States. We must reduce the enormous number of regulations that are strangling our economy. We must also provide incentives for corporations and business to stay or relocate in United States if we are to regain the level of manufacturing employment achieved in the past. All of these actions are long past due. It is partially because of our lack of attention to these issues in the past that we are experiencing the economic problems of today.

This is not a time for the United States to rely only on these programs. The process will take too much time before we can increase global employment. The employment achieved by these efforts will be insignificant in the near term. This idea demonstrates the unwillingness of many officials to recognize the urgency and magnitude of the needs of the people that can only be met by restoring global employment.

Our economic recovery plan should not be designed to find ways to compete with other nations for the sale of consumer products.

It is not the time to start an economic battle between nations to determine which nation can increase their share of the Gross Domestic Product (GDP) of the world at the expense of other nations who are struggling desperately to increase their employment also.

It is time for the more industrialized nations to recognize the plight of billions of people who are starving. It is time for leadership and cooperation with other nations to establish a new economic development paradigm which will increase the GDP of all nations.

This is the new leadership role that must be assumed by the more industrialized counties. It is time for the industrialized nations to institute an entirely new cooperative effort for global economic development to help all nations increase their employment level.

A new path to prosperity must be established for the emerging economies that will result in millions of jobs being established. We must build more peaceful relationships between all nations, reduce economic disparity and finally, establish trade agreements that are viable.

Now is the time for the people of the United States of America to step forward and lead this effort. It cannot be accomplished unless we are at the forefront, willing to pledge our time and fortunes to freeing the billions of people who are economically enslaved. They are held in economic bondage by a lack of protected private property rights and the ability to borrow funds to purchase a home.

Globalization, the economic development plan of the past, was designed to finance manufacturing in emerging economies. However, it only established low paying jobs for the manufacture of exports with no measureable prosperity for the participating nation. It was a seriously flawed concept from the beginning that failed. This new plan is designed to actually create prosperous people and avoid corruption while increasing the viable trade that globalization was intended to accomplish.

It is unlikely that the United States economy will recover again according to the old home building paradigm. It is extremely important that we not wait. Hundreds of millions of jobs must be created in emerging economies as soon as possible. This will also increase the level of employment in the more industrialized economies.

For those living in one of the more industrialized economies, it is important to recognize the seriousness of the economic problems now. Do not wait to act. The magnitude of these problems provides ample data that proves we are in a major economic depression that may turn into a global economic disaster. The major needs of the current number of product consumers have largely been met over the last few years. Meeting their reduced needs and desires are not sufficient to raise manufacturing levels back to normal.

The oversupply of consumer goods and the decrease in their global demand has resulted in too many workers and too few jobs. The current annual demand for products has decreased substantially since 2007 while the manufacturing capacity has expanded.

The actual number of the unemployed in the United States is continuing to increase. The **US Department of Labor, Bureau of Labor** announced unemployment was over twelve million in May 2012.

There is a lack of demand for new homes in the United States; it is not possible currently to begin a new housing construction cycle that would increase the demand for consumer products as it has in the past. Without a major increase in the number of new homes sales, construction unemployment will be very limited and the economy will continue to decline in spite of government stimulus programs. However, under the proposed new plan, it is possible to build millions of new homes and communities annually in emerging economies. This will establish hundreds of millions of new jobs and increase the number of new product consumers which will increase demands on manufacturing globally.

The number one priority for the leadership of every nation, seeking to increase the prosperity of their people, must be to study and adopt this new economic development plan, which creates jobs and enables the people who qualify for a home loan to invest in its purchase.

HOME BUILDING ECONOMICS

Making mortgage loans to people has proven to be the only viable method for increasing the net worth of people struggling to become prosperous. Increasing net worth through home ownership is the key to increasing the prosperity of all people.

Prosperity improves when a nation enables the people to secure a home loan. The homebuyers pull into the present a portion of their earnings from over the next thirty years and spend the entire amount on a new home in one year. When this is done by millions of people, year after year, enormous amounts of money are inserted into the emerging economies.

Billions of dollars spent annually on home construction will energize the economies year after year as millions of new homes are constructed requiring millions of new workers in all sectors of the economy. The needs of the newly employed increases the demands for consumer products which is the driving force for expanding manufacturing employment. Increasing the consumer's ability to purchase goods and services is the basis of prosperous nations and is not possible by any other method of financing.

Widespread manufacturing employment, necessary for eradicating poverty, can only be established as a response to an increase in the demand for new consumer products and services by the people. Those working in a home building industry spend the money received from the disbursement of funds from thirty year term home loans. This dramatically increases demand for consumer products as the money moves through the domestic and international economies turning over and over in the purchase of construction materials and consumer goods.

The major manufacturing economies need millions of new consumers making demands for new products in order to increase manufacturing employment. The emerging countries need jobs so that their people are enabled to become product consumers to purchase their daily needs. Establishing an economic development program that will meet the needs of both crises will usher in a new economic era based on cooperation between nations, not aggressive competition.

The large employment base in the home building industry in the United States is the driving force that creates the demand for manufactured consumer products which has increased employment to levels not achievable by other methods. When the number of homes being constructed each year is on the rise, the United States economy expands and prosperity increases. When the demand for housing declines the economy slows and there is unemployment. If you are trying to increase the prosperity in your country, you must understand home building economics.

You may believe that manufacturing employment created prosperity in the United States; it is simply not true. You cannot make a major increase in manufacturing employment without a major increase in the demand for consumer products. The housing industry provides people with the means to create a demand for consumer products far in excess of what can be achieved with the discretionary income from a manufacturing job. People spend home loan proceeds and energize the economy. This is the unequivocal reason the United States has became the most prosperous nation on the planet.

Establishing a home building industry in emerging economies that have become politically and economically free will create enormous prosperity and eradicate poverty just as it did in the United States.

LACK OF LEADERSHIP - ECONOMIC TURMOIL

It is necessary that this book concentrate only on the issues relating to the plan for creating jobs. However, a brief overview of the economic turmoil in the United States helps to explain why it is necessary to invest in the development of housing in emerging economies if we are to reenergize our economy.

Unaware of how the new domestic and international economic forces are altering the global economy in recent years, elected officials have continued to create and approve irresponsible budgets while recognizing that unemployment was increasing as housing demand slowed.

Government budgets were adopted in the past based on the assumption that it was permissible to borrow whatever was needed. No one anticipated that the economy might not recover. The tax revenues have been insufficient because the economy has not following the typical cycle. This economic attitude at all levels of government can no longer be permitted under the changing global economic demands.

New representatives must be sought out and elected that have the experience and knowledge to manage the expenditures of government in a viable manner while recognizing the changing global economic conditions. The size of many government agencies must be reduced and some must be eliminated. Regulations that retard investments and formation of new businesses must be terminated. Much of the federal authority to address the problems must be returned to the state level.

Problems must be addressed at the lowest possible level of representation and managed in detail by people closer to the local problems. We need more experienced and knowledgeable representatives if a new economic plan is to be implemented.

We are being crushed with debt at the federal and state levels because of a lack of competent leadership. Inexperienced elected officials did not consider it prudent to establish reserves in anticipation of lower tax revenues even while unemployment was increasing. In an attempt to revitalize the economy and increase tax revenue, more funds were borrowed and spent without any real understanding of the economic problems. These resulted in no substantial improvement in employment and the economy.

Economists are warning that if the debts of the federal and state governments in the United States continue to increase, there is potential for a major financial disruption if the governments are unable to borrow sufficiently to service the debt.

An inability to make payments could bankrupt the nation and destroy the economy. There is no government plan being proposed to increase employment and tax revenues sufficiently to address these problems.

It appears that the seriousness of the over spending has been greatly underestimated by those in power. They have failed to recognize what impact overspending and increasing the debt would have on the future of our economy and future generations if the economy cannot be restored to former levels.

Without any real understanding of the reasons for the unemployment problems, money was borrowed and spent on programs that did not relate to the causes of the problems. The programs were doomed to fail.

The United States is experiencing an increase in inflation and the dollar is weakening. Budget fights are breaking out. Should programs be cut to match revenue or to increase the debt limits? Should we continue to borrow in order to provide what we can no longer afford? Contracts are being honored despite the fact that the tax payers do not have the money to pay for government commitments and contracts which should be terminated.

The budget fights are a result of elected officials in the past not bothering to understand the need to prepare carefully planned budgets. This attitude at all levels of government can no longer be permitted. Other problems not addressed properly in the past have added to the problems. Here are a few.

IMMIGRATION AND EXPORTING JOBS

Elected officials are unwilling to address the laws that prevent people from finding jobs. These laws are increasing the number of those seeking the limited number of jobs in the United States, while at the same time reducing the number of jobs available. There are laws allowing one million legal immigrants to be added to our population each year. We are permitting manufacturing jobs to be exported and the products produced by those jobs established overseas to be imported.

If these trends are not altered by a new plan for economic development, this global crisis will grow for many years and could lead to a catastrophe, not only for the United States but also for those that depend on our prosperous economy. Unemployment will continue to increase and wages will continue to decline if there is not a change in the direction of the flow of migrant workers.

We also must find a way for the remaining manufacturers to compete with low cost imports. It may be difficult to understand why the proposed plan will resolve the problems without recognizing and understanding how this situation was allowed to develop and how it has impacted the global economy.

EFFORTS TO REDUCE IMMIGRATION

NumbersUSA, a non-profit, non-partisan, public policy organization located in Arlington, Virginia, provides projections of trends on immigration based on census data to the general public. The charts on their website project the trend in legal immigration as a result of our current laws that specify the number of legal immigrants permitted to enter the United States annually.

NumbersUSA's publications raise issues being created by legal and illegal immigration that are not being discussed in the media. They have projected the total population in 2070 will exceed five hundred million, an increase of two hundred million.

Their website, NumbersUSA.com, quoting U.S. Census data, reports that since 1970 the number of legal immigrants to the United States (and their subsequent descendents) has grown to fifty million, in 2011.

If we continue to allow legal immigration at the current rate, the total number of legal immigrants will be over one hundred and fifty million by the year 2070, including the current fifty million immigrants and descendents already here. That number does not include illegal immigrants and descendents.

Roy Beck and his people at NumbersUSA have been lobbying for years to lower legal immigration levels because they believe that the high rate of legal immigration creates a potentially dangerous situation for the United States economy and the economies of other countries dependent on our purchase of imports.

When the number of illegal immigrants is added to their projections of the legal immigrant work force, it illustrates the immediate crisis that we are experiencing. It will be impossible to create sufficient jobs to support a population growth of 200 million people over the next sixty years based on the current economic paradigm which is failing to create new jobs.

Millions of foreign workers are forced to flee their native country in their efforts to find jobs to support and feed their families. Finding a more humane solution to the problems of a lack of jobs and hunger in the poor countries must become a priority for all nations concerned about the extreme poverty in the world.

The *International Organization for Migration's World Migration Report* estimates that there were two hundred and fourteen million migrants in 2010 living abroad.

The 164 million immigrants in Western Europe are creating unemployment and a major budget crisis in a number of countries.

According to **Human Events, The National Conservative Weekly**, Greece, Ireland, and Portugal are being bailed out by loans from the International Monetary Fund, (IMF) and Spain and Italy are already borrowing to stay afloat.

The level of the United States funding of the IMF increased from approximately $10 trillion pre-2009 to $105 trillion post 2009. The IMF stated that the United States debt problems are creating a crisis in the value of its currency. It is doubtful that the United States can afford to borrow more money to loan to other countries.

At the current rate of increase, if the global unemployment trend continues, the total immigrants needing jobs in the more industrialized countries worldwide will exceed 850 million by the year 2060. At present, there are no plans in the works that will prevent this from happening or identify the source of the funds needed for future bailouts. Tragically, past loans to governments in the form of bailouts have largely been failures because they did not address the enormous unemployment problem. The proposed plan is a humane solution to the problem. Employment in emerging countries solves many problems.

THE CLOSE OF AN ERA

Increased immigration and low cost imports have brought the economic system in the United States to a point referred to as the closing of the "*Economic Golden Era*" by the *Journal of Economic Literature*.

During the period from 1924 to 1965, a period of low immigration, all Americans experienced the greatest increase in real incomes. However, there are now too many workers in the United States and other developed countries with too few job opportunities, hence the buying power of lower wages has declined. Our major cities are experiencing increasing demands for human services for the unemployed.

The percentage of people in middle income groups is much smaller now than when the number of manufacturing jobs was expanding and there were ample job opportunities.

The empirical data on job losses during recent years indicates that if we fail to address the forces impacting wages, we are destined to suffer a serious global economic decline as unemployment continues and wages fall. Falling wages reduces the demand for consumer goods because there is less discretionary income. It is now appropriate to declare the Economic Golden Era officially over.

THE HIGH COST OF UNEMPLOYMENT BENEFITS

The most significant problem contributing to governments exceeding budgets is this over-supply of labor.

Qualified and experienced people are unable to find work. People are being forced to draw on unemployment benefits, the last thing they ever thought would happen to them.

People in serious trouble have driven up the cost of unemployment benefits, health care, welfare, and education. This has become an incredible burden for our governments and other governments internationally.

Excessive borrowing and spending just to meet budget demands and entitlements has further undermined our economy.

When unemployment became a problem, legislation was passed in an attempt to solve the economic crisis by borrowing and increasing the debt to fund these programs instead of reducing the size of government and limiting immigration to increase the availability of jobs.

This has resulted in a dilemma. What is the best way to help those that are starving in the emerging economies? Should we increase immigration when we have no jobs? Would it be more humane to create more jobs in emerging economies and reverse immigration to fill jobs in their native countries?

FOOD STAMPS – GOVERNMENT FOOD PROGRAMS

The government has reported that the number of people without the money to buy food is one out of seven people and increasing. They are now receiving food stamps. The economy continues to struggle while tax revenues have dropped and are no longer sufficient to meet budget spending. We have a stalled economy with high unemployment, governments that are too large, out of control debt, and people that have no money for food.

The number of recipients on food stamps in 2009 was 28 million. According to the **USDA *Food and Nutrition Service's Food Stamp Participation Report***, in January of 2011, the number of people using food stamps was still increasing. There are now approximately 44 million people on food stamps in the United States alone. The food stamp programs cost federal taxpayers $56 billion in fiscal 2009, triple the $18 billion cost in fiscal 2000. Federal spending on the two food programs that provide free and low-cost breakfast and lunch meals was an additional $16 billion in fiscal 2009.

This covers 80,000 public schools and 30 million children. People are starving because our leadership does not understand the problem. People prefer jobs to food stamps.

SOCIAL SECURITY IN UNITED STATES

Social Security funds held by the United States government are now being discussed as if the account was an entitlement, and it is appropriate to reduce payments in an effort to balance the federal budget. Social Security was not set up as a retirement account to be disbursed by the government. It was established as a reserve for the security of people when Franklin Delano Roosevelt was president in the event of another depression. The money belongs to the people who contributed to the account. The contributed money was taken out of people's wages.

Unlike other security programs in other nations, the United States Social Security system is not separate from the federal government and can be raided by elected officials if they deem it is necessary.

Elected officials approved appropriating the funds and depositing the money in the general account to be spent to cover operating costs many years ago. This was not legal. The government issued promissory notes for the funds. The notes today have little value if the government is unable to borrow more money to pay off the notes.

The Social Security system must now rely on the government to borrow funds or print money to pay off notes and put money back into the Social Security system to pay the people monthly because there is a deficit budget.

This will undoubtedly mean that if the economy crashes, Social Security will not receive adequate payments from the government because it will no longer be able to borrow the funds to repay Social Security.

To restore the money to the account, other programs favored by the politicians will have to be cut. Social Security will be forced to reduce or stop payments if those elected do not cut programs they have already promised to their contributors. Fifty-three million Americans in the United States receive social security benefits that are used to pay basic living expenses at a great benefit to the economy. Non-payment or a major reduction in the benefits would add to the already seriousness of the crisis.

HIGHER REVENUE REQUIRED TO SERVICE THE LARGER DEBT

When the seriousness of the slowdown in the economy is fully appreciated and understood, it becomes obvious that we are not just experiencing another recession because housing was over built and there is little demand for new homes. There are basic changes in the demand and supply of consumer goods that are altering the employment pattern globally.

It is not economically feasible to survive this crisis without a major increase in the number of new consumers. The lack of demand for consumer products is creating the unemployment. We have to adopt a new global plan to create new jobs that will increase the tax revenue above the level reached in the past. The increase in revenues must be sufficient to meet the needs of the budgets and to repay a $14 trillion dollar debt. It does not appear that anyone is proposing a plan to accomplish this herculean task.

In a normal cycle, we recover from an economic slowdown when housing demand increases and construction begins. Because of the oversupply in homes and the slow increase in the number of new home buyers, it is not likely that there will be an increase in home building that will sufficiently increase the tax revenue to pay off the debt in the short term.

The population growth pattern is not producing another wave of home buyers like the one that caused the last home building boom. It takes an increase in home building and its related employment to create an increase in demands for consumer products. If there is no substantial increase in consumer demands, manufacturing cannot employ more people.

The seriousness of the debt and the lack of demand for consumer goods suddenly become overwhelming. To revitalize the economy to its former vitality, the increase in the economy must greatly surpass past levels of GDP if the tax rates are to remain the same or reduced.

Much higher tax revenues at the federal and state level are required to provide the amount of funds needed for the normal operation of governments and additional revenue to service the enormous debt payments. This plan has the ability to create the larger national GDP when implemented on a scale sufficient to construct the millions of homes that are needed.

Elected officials have not provided any evidence that they understand the amount of the increase in the GDP and the total revenue that will be required to return to the same level of prosperity and pay off the debt. This higher level of prosperity requires a new unique approach to the establishment of a global economic development plan.

Failing to create a new robust economy will force future generations to live a less prosperous life with less net revenue for government services until the debt is removed. Unless something is done quickly, the children of the future will inherit bankrupt countries.

GLOBALIZATION

Under the previous global economic development strategy attempted by the IMF and the World Bank, in cooperation with the international banking community, the economies of the borrowing countries were not improved even to a level that provided sufficient tax revenue for repayment of the loans.

The plan was an approach to economic development that took the money from the people of one country and gave it to the governments of struggling countries.

The money did not pass through the hands of the people nor did it create consumer demands. We have experienced several global economic crises because of the failure of several countries to repay the loans from the IMF. The IMF officials making the loans had no understanding of how to increase the prosperity of a nation, yet they were placed in charge to do exactly that.

At the same time, immigration was adding millions of workers to manufacturing economies that did not need more workers; no effort was made to protect manufacturers from the importation of less expensive imports by foreign competition created by globalization.

Manufacturing companies were forced to move their operations from the more industrialized countries to the emerging economies where there were lower labor rates, no corporate income taxes, and less bureaucratic burdens. Many corporations would have failed if they had not found a way to compete with the increase in importation of competitive and less expensive consumer goods, while, at the same time, wages were increasing according to contractual commitments.

The rapid increase in the importation of low cost goods was partially caused by new countries with low wages being permitted to join the World Trade Organization.

Their newly emerging manufacturers became major exporters by underbidding other exporters such as the United States, the EU, and China. In the United States the willingness of elected officials to help other countries to become prosperous by not imposing tariffs on imports became the national priority ahead of the welfare of its own people.

United States companies relocate their plants to foreign countries to avoid paying U.S. corporate income and property taxes. They do not pay taxes on corporate income in foreign countries or export taxes when shipping their products back to the United States. Elected officials ignored the long term consequences of permitting low cost imports on employment in the more industrialized countries.

A recent University of California at Berkeley report projected another 14 million jobs are at risk of being moved offshore.

China reported the loss of twenty-five million manufacturing jobs in one year. Many of the manufacturers that relocated in countries that became new members of the WTO began to under-price China's exports.

Unemployment increased and factories were closed. In response to the reduction of exports, China established private property rights and stepped up the home building industry to restore their annual rate of increase in Gross Domestic Product (GDP).

TRADE DEFICIT

The "Open Door" was the economic policy of the day when this all started.

During the early expansion of our manufacturing base in the 1950s, we were the major exporter. Because there were no tariffs imposed on low cost imports, the manufacturing labor force in the United States began to fall when no action was taken to prevent it.

The manufacturing labor force was over 33% of the total labor force in the United States when the economy was expanding fifty years ago.

The manufacturing labor force is now less than 12% of a total work force of approximately 154 million. This has lead to a lower paid middle class which is growing in size. Currently, we import more than twice what we export.

The trade deficit in International Goods and Services was over six hundred billion dollars in 2010 according to a ***Central Intelligence Agency's Report*** on international trade.

The trade deficit is roughly $2,000 per capita. This means every man, woman and child in United States sends $2,000 to foreign countries in support of their economy each year. Think about the number of jobs $600 billion in purchases of consumer products would have done for the business community if the consumer products had been purchased in United States.

THE COMPOUNDING OF THE PROBLEM

As a result of the loss of jobs, there has also been a drop in tax revenue. This increases the budget problems. At the same time the cost of government programs and entitlements continues to increase due to mandated services and contracted commitments.

Almost without notice the contracted salaries and benefits of those employed in government and education have continued to rise while the private sector wages have declined. It is now obvious that we may not be able to fund employee contracts if we don't find a solution for revitalizing our economy. Our borrowing and spending economy is on the verge of collapsing.

"NO THANKS I'VE GOT ONE"

For over sixty years, the industrialized countries have been expanding the global manufacturing capacity to meet the increase in the demands of a growing population. This rapidly expanding employment produced a large affluent class at all income levels in many countries. This new group of employees and their families, approximately 30% of the world's population, created a tremendous demand for consumer products.

The current demand for more consumer products has now declined. As a result, the manufacturing volume has been reduced. This is the cause of the current worldwide unemployment crisis. The needs and demands of the product consumer class have changed and are not sufficient to support the capacity of the current global manufacturing industry. Most of us know people who have adopted the attitude, "*No thanks, I've got one.*" in response to advertisements promoting sales.

After the spending frenzy of the past few years, sales have slowed and retail stores and manufacturers have closed. Store sales are down because of the decrease in demand for normal consumer goods such as appliances, TVs, automobiles, and clothes. The global unemployment crisis was unequivocally caused by the current lack of demand for consumer products which is not going to change in the near term.

With most of the consumer needs met, it is unlikely that this is just a normal recession that will correct itself.

There were simply more new automobiles, TVs, computers, phones, clothing, and other products being manufactured than approximately two billion people have the need, or even the desire to purchase.

For example in 2009, fourteen million cars were scrapped while only 10 million new cars were sold in United States. Growing unemployment is contributing to the lack of consumer demand.

The reduction in imports is also impacting the unaddressed level of global poverty which is now increasing even more rapidly than in prior years.

The solution to this unemployment crisis is to establish a global home building industry in the emerging economies to build millions of modern quality homes. Home building will create millions of jobs in real estate development and construction that will in turn create jobs in all sectors of the global economy. We must stop experimenting with government stimulus programs that are not economically sound and begin to create jobs using standard private sectors means.

It is now clear why the more industrialized economies cannot recover to the former levels of prosperity under the old paradigm for development.

The major portion of the demand has been met. We must adopt a new economic development plan addresses the changes in the laws that are necessary in the governing process and economic relations globally.

This will free us from current limitations and create an entirely new global economic development environment that will create manufacturing jobs globally and reduce economic disparity.

A MORE HUMANE SOLUTION

Global efforts to assist the poor in emerging economies have permitted millions of immigrants to join the work forces of the more industrialized nations; at the same time, the supply of jobs has declined as corporations moved to countries with lower wages. If there had been an understanding of what was happening with the global economy, these efforts could have addressed the root cause of the unemployment problem and offered a much better solution.

A more practical and humane approach would have been to establish an economic development plan that would actually create jobs in the emerging economies and help the people to become more prosperous in their own land. There would be greater opportunities for upward mobility if they were enabled to work and own a home in their native land. This approach would have eliminated the suffering of billions of people years ago. Many people in their search for food and housing died when forced to flee their native country to find work and feed their families. But it is not too late to do the right thing and help each nation become prosperous and independent.

This is not a recession! We are experiencing a major crisis! There are larger problems than those created by the over building of homes and the financial mismanagement. From all of the indications, the facts and statistics indicate that we are entering a major crisis because of our lack of understanding of the changing needs of the world. What we need is a plan that will create a large source of revenue if we are going to pay off our debts and make loans to help revitalize the global economy.

It must be a plan that will create an increased global demand for consumer products in order to expand global manufacturing employment and our level of economic activity to a much higher level. Spending trillions of dollars building homes around the world to meet the needs of the growing population will create a demand for consumer products globally for years into the future.

PART IV

POVERTY - THE OTHER CRISIS

If we are to reduce economic disparity, achieve global prosperity, and establish peace for all people, the world needs to finance a new population of product consumers. This will increase consumer demands and establish a major increase in global employment for the present and into the future reducing economic disparity between nations and begin the process of eradicating global poverty.

OBEDIENCE TO
THE RULES OF PROPSERITY

The current economic problems started in the 1940s when the economies of some nations began to expand rapidly for the first time. Because of a lack of economic freedom, the poorest countries began to fall behind and could not keep pace. The rapidly expanding industrial base created a whole new class of working people who became prosperous while over 60% of the world population was held in economic bondage due to a lack of rights. The struggling nations also attempted to create an industrialized base, but a necessary principle for creating prosperity was not being adhered to in the development of their economies.

Some of the countries that fell behind were controlled by tyrants and dictators only interested in their own economic gain. The leaders made no attempt to create an economy where people were able to work and become prosperous themselves. Many of those in power financed themselves and the economy by selling their countries natural resources and made little or no attempt to actually create an industrious and prosperous nation while they stayed in power.

As the years passed, the lack of jobs and the subsequent increase in poverty created a condition of economic disparity between nations.

This has become the cause of much of the stress between nations and the driving force creating the current global economic crisis and unemployment.

Creating housing was not considered a major need of their people. Since then, millions of people have been forced to immigrate to find work in order to feed their families. Others have recently decided to revolt and form new governments in an attempt to establish democracy and prosperity for everyone. For emerging nations striving to achieve democratic freedom, there is a need for millions of jobs. They have to learn about building new housing to create jobs.

ECONOMIC DISPARITY
BETWEEN NATIONS

To create jobs according to the proposed economic development plan, each nation will have to establish protected private property rights and other laws similar to those of other nations who have achieved a high level of prosperity. Frankly, I was unaware how serious the economic disparity had become until I was on one of my trips in the early 1990s into the mountains of Peru. I experienced a close-up view of severe poverty for the first time when I witnessed hundreds of thousands of families living in junk yards and temporary shelters scattered throughout a desert valley.

It was during a time when we were developing a housing project for a new copper mine in the Andes.

As a consequence of this life changing experience, I decided to undertake a study to determine what economic and political limitations were holding hundreds of millions of men, women, and children captives in such an inhumane existence. It turned out that the number was much larger than I thought.

I began to study the laws and economics of many emerging economies and discovered that economic disparity with each country has continued to increase to the present day. There are billions of people on this earth that are not significant buyers of consumer products. The World Bank 2005 statistics show that over four billion men, women and children are attempting to live on $2.50 per day. (PPP) This is the upper tier international poverty line used by the World

Bank. This is more than half of the world's population of six billion, nine hundred million.

Of that amount two billion, six hundred million live below the World Bank's second tier international poverty line of $2.00 per day (PPP). Lowering the poverty line again, the number of people living on less than $1.25 per day (PPP) exceeds one billion-three hundred million.

These numbers are still growing in many countries because of the increase in the price of commodities and food.

Unemployment is on the rise again due to the reduction in demand for consumer products in the global economy.

The remaining population of approximately 2.8 billion people on this earth live in luxury unimaginable 60 years ago in comparison to the over four billion that are living in various levels of poverty.

Today, according to the *World Institute for Development Economics Research at United Nations University,* 10% of all adults account for 85% of the world's assets. It is even more alarming if we assume that by "all adults," they are referring to approximately 30% of the total population that are adults; 10% of 30% means that 3% of the world's population accounts for 85% of the worlds assets.

What is terrifying about this is that some of these same people want to wage war on others just to increase their wealth. Some of these wealthy people want to subjugate countries by bringing them under the control of what they refer to as a "One World Government."

This increasing economic disparity between and within nations is what is creating global stress between nations. Many are now erupting in revolutions. At the same time, there are no jobs being established to meet the needs of the people.

In the past, with the type of aid programs that were implemented for struggling countries, it was difficult to establish a means for the people to work and increase their level of prosperity.

These were wonderful programs that reduced some suffering, but they did not address the problems creating poverty and increasing economic disparity.

The average GDP per capita of the more industrialized nations has now grown to more than twenty times that of the struggling economies. In the United States, the GDP per Capita is over $47,000. Compare this to many of the developing economies where it is approximately $2,000 per capita. This disparity in income has created major international shifts in the employment base.

Economic disparity is the force imposing incredible financial burdens on all countries and limiting the growth of the emerging economies.

The increasing economic disparity can only be reversed by the adoption of an international economic development plan that will enable the eventual eradication of severe poverty and dramatically increase the number of jobs in all struggling economies by increasing consumer demand. All nations must support this plan.

The lack of employment for the impoverished has resulted in enormous health problems, epidemics, needless deaths, and devastating hunger. Billions of people live in shanties and temporary shelters in all countries, rich and poor. Unfortunately, this merciless state of living for billions continues to be ignored by those who have the power to make changes, but do not know how to create jobs.

This is at a time when people and financial institutions in the more prosperous nations have capital that is languishing for the lack of viable investments. The more prosperous nations and their global economic institutions have the knowledge and the wealth to free billions of people from economic slavery and their inhumane existence. All they must do is adopt this plan as the number one global priority. It is a viable solution. There is no alternative to reducing economic disparity and increasing global prosperity. It can be accomplished by investing in housing in emerging economies.

Approximately two billion of the more affluent population is not consuming products at the previous rate and approximately four billion have purchased little or nothing in the way of consumer products. The logical solution would be to convert those that are not part of the consumer demand class to consumers with demands for consumer products.

The August 6, 2010 issue of *The Economist,* a London based magazine, specializing in economic news worldwide, made the observation; "What the world lacks is willing customers, not willing workers."

However, it is not enough to recognize that this is what is needed for increasing employment globally. It is impossible to have new consumers who have money to buy products without first creating jobs for them so they can become willing workers.

That is the importance of financing home building in emerging economies; to create jobs and demands for consumer products. The financing of housing in emerging economies introduces trillions of dollars into the global economy. It is the solution to the global unemployment problem.

A STALLING GLOBAL ECONOMY

My first book published in 2007, *A Home for Every Family*, also proposed a worldwide home building industry. The book pointed out the many signs that the world was headed for serious unemployment. Reduced consumer demands were already appearing and indicated that we needed more product consumers. Current signs indicate that the more developed economies will continue to slide until the cause of the unemployment problem is resolved. In many countries exports are down and domestic employment cannot be increased.

Most of the members of the European Union need jobs to get out of debt. Western stock market investors are painfully aware of the lack of attractive investment opportunities, while markets in India, Southeast Asia, and China do not show great promise for investments because of global unemployment.

Major American corporations have closed factories and fired thousands of employees. Some have seen their stock downgraded to "junk" status.

The value of most large corporate stocks is questionable at best because of attempts to increase the bottom line through corporate shrinkage, stock buybacks and slashing prices to encourage people to buy.

Banks around the world are having difficulty finding suitable lending opportunities. The banks have encouraged people to buy homes they could not afford. Homeowners were encouraged to borrow home equity loans. The excessive borrowing created a major loss of homes for those that could not make the payments in a slowing economy.

Home equity loans made as a second loan subordinated the first mortgage on the assets of the homeowner. This was intended to provide funds for the homeowner to spend which would increase consumer demand for products.

Unfortunately, it increased consumer debt per person to an unmanageable level and then the demand died.

It was not the correct solution to reviving a slowing global economy.

Financing a global home building industry will restore the global economy when the home loans are made based on standard lending terms concerning equity and income.

FOUR BILLION LIVING IN POVERTY NOW

The poor are seriously neglected on our planet. Everyday people are suffering with no hope that they can improve their lives.

The total number of men at 10% of the population is 400,000,000 that need jobs or better jobs. Everyday people are dying, including millions of children, because of our indifference. It is very difficult to imagine the number of lives that are at stake. Most of us on this planet have watched a sporting event on television where 40,000 people are crowded into a stadium. Imagine a stadium filled with poor men, women, and children stricken with poverty and disease.

Would that be a sight that would stick in your memory? Because of the high rate of deaths, some would die while you are looking at the vision.

It would take 1,000 stadiums filled with 40,000 people each to hold just 40,000,000 people.

Now visualize 100,000 stadiums each filled with 40,000 poor and starving women, men and children which would be the number required to hold the four billion people now living under inhumane condition; well over 50% of them live under the poverty limit. What a horrible vision. Think about 60% of the people on this planet living on less than $2.50 per day.

Every source tends to report different numbers, but they all provide an indication of the seriousness of worldwide poverty. The following data has been taken from the ISSUES section of Anup Shan's Website:
www.globalissues.org/article/26/povery-facts-and-stats.

There are at least one billion children living in poverty. This is almost 50% of all children. There are 640 million children without adequate shelter.

There are 400 million children with no access to safe water and there are 270 million children with no access to health services. According to UNICEF, 24,000 children die each day due to unhealthy living condition. In 2003, 10.6 million children died before they reached 5 years of age and the trend is increasing today.

Current numbers are worse because the emerging economies are declining due to global unemployment.

Children are suffering and dying while their parents struggle to find work and food. These people are people just like you and me. They have the same dreams as all people do while thinking that no one cares about their existence.

THREE BILLION MORE PEOPLE BY 2050

In 1960, 20% of the world's population in the richest countries had 30 times the income of the poorest 20%. By 1997 this had increased to 74 times.

It is easy to see what the future holds for billions of people if we do not act now to stop this trend. Conditions continue to get worse as the population increases because the poor do not have an economic system which actually produces prosperity for all people.

The situation becomes much worse when you consider that some projections indicate that the global population of 6.8 billion could increase by three billion over the next forty years to a total of 9.8 billion in 2050.

This number is an estimated average of several scenarios. It could be higher if the health services improve.

EL SALVADOR SETTING THE EXAMPLE

El Salvador is now on the path to prosperity. A complete renewal has emerged since the civil conflict which almost destroyed the country in 1992.

It has adopted many of the suggestions made in this economic development plan. El Salvador adopted the U.S. dollar as its official currency. According to the Center for Global Liberty & Prosperity (CATO Institute, Washington, D.C.) in their March 9, 2009 No. 8

report by Juan Carlos Hidalgo, they have turned to privatizing the state enterprises, deregulation of businesses, less controls on trade, and financial liberalization. They have privatized the pension system which is the accepted method for establishing retirement funds in many emerging economies.

El Salvador now ranks among the top 25 freest economies in the world according to the Fraser Institute's, *Economic Freedom of the World Report.* It's GDP per capita grew to over $6,500 by 2007 and yet the lack of security and violence continue to be a problem.

Many of the people do not have a stake in the economy and are locked out of participating in the economic growth. Establishing an opportunity to become economically free by creating laws that enable home ownership provides a stake in the future and holds the promise that conditions will improve for all.

HOME BUILDING IN MEXICO

Mexico is establishing a home building industry that is setting an example for Latin America countries. Numerous companies in the United States, such as the California Public Employees Retirement System are already financing projects in Mexico.

Well-established mortgage insurers such as Glenworth Financial and AIG United Guaranty are already backing Mexican loans.

In 2008, President Felipe Calderon set a national goal for all of Mexico to fund one million new mortgages by 2010. As of the summer of 2011, the Instituto Del Fondo Nacional de la Vivenda (Infonavit), Mexico's Federal Housing Fund was on track to fund well over 800,000. Mexico has projected a need for 15 million new dwelling units to meet current demands. Each year there is a new demand for at least 800,000 new units. In the past only six percent of the 25.7 million homes were financed with mortgages. Delinquency rates have been reported below 4%.

LATIN AMERICA HOUSING FINANCE SUMMIT

At the Latin American Housing Summit meeting held in February, 2008, in Florida, it was reported that Latin American's housing deficit may be as high as 54 million homes.

Representatives from Wall Street firms, international finance companies, banking representatives from all over Latin America, development banks and INFONAVIT attended the summit.

The increase in demand for real estate and the increasing interest in growth have started the process of meeting the needs of hundreds of millions of people in Latin America.

The increase in the use of structured financing tools is developing rapidly, making demands for more regulatory changes. Securitization is now considered a viable option. The idea of international mortgage insurance is accepted as a tool for reducing lender risks when the international agreements provide for the protection of all parties.

HOW MANY HOMES ARE NEEDED GLOBALLY

There are billions of people that are homeless or living in substandard housing with no safe water, waste disposal, or electricity. Should this plan for a global home building industry be adopted, there would be a requirement to house 4.0 billion people initially. This would take many years even at an accelerated pace. The number of new modern homes required assuming four people per household could be as high as 1.0 billion.

The increase in population is projected to be another three billion by 2050. This creates an additional requirement for at least 750 million homes at four people per household.

The increase in the number of development and construction jobs over the years will be enormous and the newly employed will create the demand for consumer goods that will support manufacturing job worldwide.

Initially home loans are made to the working people and the affluent that qualify. As construction starts, the newly employed in this new industry and its related services become qualified to purchase a new modern standard quality home. Affordable homes or starter homes would not be constructed.

This is the process that has been used for creating national employment and homes in the United States for over sixty years.

The capital required to provide adequate housing for 7 billion people over the next 50 to 60 years would be enormous. This approach to creating jobs provides the answer to the question of how we eradicate poverty now and prevent it from reoccurring as the population dramatically increases over the coming years.

PART V

TWELVE ECONOMIC PRINCIPLES
THAT CREATE PROSPEROUS PEOPLE

Financing and organizing a home building industry in every emerging economy where the leaders are dedicated to the welfare and freedom of its people is the only economic development plan that creates millions of jobs and establishes prosperity for all of the people.

NEW PRODUCT CONSUMERS

There are over four billion people not making a significant demand for consumer products, waiting now for the opportunity to work and become product consumers. There are 2 billion people living on less than $2.US per day for food, medicine, housing, and clothing. There are actually close to 4 billion people out of the 6.9 billion on this planet that are not able to purchase even their basic needs. Creating jobs in emerging economies will reduce economic disparity between the emerging economies and the more industrialized countries which will reduce many of the problems in international trade. Establishing jobs for those in need will create additional product consumers, making a global demand for manufactured products of over four billion people or approximately twice the current number of major consumers. This increases employment in the more industrialized economies as the demand for consumer products increases in the emerging economies.

HOW TO CREATE JOBS
FOR THE UNEMPLOYED

The answer is to develop homes in emerging economies in the same manner as is done in the United States.

The loan process inserts money into their economy, creating millions of new construction jobs and consumers demanding new products.

The infusion of the funds into their economy from construction will create millions of jobs in all sectors of the economy, reduce poverty, and eliminate the need for families to migrate in the search of jobs. When their economies begin to expand, there will be a need for millions of skilled and educated immigrants to return to the countries of origin to lead and take part in the new opportunities.

THE SOLUTION

This is a new global economic development plan for adopting and internationalizing the natural laws of economics that have been the driving force in successfully creating jobs and enormous prosperity in the United States. To create global prosperity a homebuilding industry must be established for the construction of homes in emerging economies which will reduce extreme poverty and global unemployment. The adoption of the home development process used in America and the establishment of an international banking and mortgage insurance system to finance the construction of an affordable home for every family in need is the key to global prosperity in the 21ST century.

The success of the plan depends on financing homes for those that are employed or are affluent and are currently living in homes at all price levels. For every new home constructed, an existing home is vacated for others to move up.

A multi-trillion dollar home construction industry building quality homes for affluent families in participating emerging economies eradicates severe poverty and creates hundreds of millions of construction jobs.

This will in turn establish an enormous demand for consumer products internationally. This is precisely what home construction has done in the United States of America for over sixty years.

The process of raising the level of income in the United States over the past fifty years is the product of millions of people borrowing money year after year based on their ability to pay it back in the future and spending the funds in one year. The result was that tens of millions of people were put to work providing the services that the funds from the home loans demand. The prosperity of the entire population is lifted as those working to provide the materials and services for the construction industry spend their earnings for other types of consumer products. It increases demand for goods which result in increasing the number of manufacturing jobs. Consumer demands for products must increase before manufacturing employment can be restored.

Prosperity will begin to increase in any country when home loans energize the economic system as people purchase an appreciating asset. The increase in home value over time begins the process that creates wealth for every family.

UNDERSTANDING ECONOMICS

Understanding the **Twelve Economic Principles That Create Prosperous People** or *Participatory Economics* is the key to eradicating prosperity. It is defined here as an economic environment established within a participatory democracy where the people are free to participate in their own economy as investors because they possess protected private property rights.

Experience in America has proven that if the working people have the opportunity to participate in their own economy by borrowing to invest in a home; it is possible for the people of any nation to become prosperous.

TWELVE ECONOMIC PRINCIPLES THAT CREATE PROSPEROUS PEOPLE

1 Private Property Rights Permit The People To Invest In Their Own Economy. Establishment of Private Property Rights for individuals and businesses is the first principle of the natural law of economics. This principle must govern the sovereignty over any nation attempting to create prosperity for its people. The key to creating prosperity is providing the clear and unequivocal right under the constitution of a nation for the people to own property. Any nation whose constitution does not provide for laws granting private property rights to its citizens prevents the people from borrowing and becoming prosperous by investing in their own economy.

 2 Judicial Rectitude Protects Private Property Rights. It is critical that private property rights be protected by the establishment and enforcement of a constitutional guarantee and the validity of legal contracts of title under the rule of the law. Precise terminology must be adopted for constitutional law and other legal documentation to eliminate ambiguous wording and reduce the number of legal conflicts that must be resolved in court. This also reduces the burden on judicial authorities in determining the rightful ownership and legal liens in the event of disputes. Reliance on the legal process both domestically and internationally is essential for the protection of the lender in extending credit to prospective home owners and for the owner when entering into contracts.

 3 Credit Worthy Borrowers Are The Homebuyers There is a financing principle that establishes the feasibility for making home loans in emerging economies. Initially the money must be loaned only to the people who qualify for a conventional loan to purchase a quality, modern home. These borrowers must have established income records that show their ability to pay the mortgage payments. This reduces the risks to lenders and the number of defaults on home loans.

Reducing risks increases the number of financial institutions willing to invest in home mortgages in developing countries. The credit worthiness of the people determines the strength of the economy of any nation where home building is the predominate industry that creates jobs. Increasing the prosperity of the nation becomes the responsibility of those with credit. These are the people who will profit most from a more prosperous economy.

Currently many of the more affluent and employed still live in homes that are far below the level that they can afford simply because of the lack of new home construction brought on by the difficulty in purchasing land and/or a lack of protected property rights and high interest rates on loans. There are also restrictions and limits on mortgage financing at practical rates of interest that prevent homes from being constructed for the working people. When this plan is implemented and homes are constructed for those who initially qualify for a loan, the development and construction of the homes will employ others who will qualify.

Thanks to studies of the magnitude of the wealth that is possessed by middle and upper income people in developing countries, there is sufficient evidence to prove that hundreds of millions of families now have sufficient net worth or income to qualify for substantial home loans.

According to Hernando De Soto's research published in his book *The Mystery of Capital*7 there are approximately $10 trillion dollars tied up in "dead capital" throughout the underdeveloped countries because of the lack of legal titles for the transfer or development of the land or business ownership. By dead capital, Mr. Soto explains that the people have equity in their assets but are unable to sell the asset or leverage the equity for buying or starting a new business or home.

There is no actual mystery concerning the capital. What are lacking are protected private property rights that free the people to buy and sell property. In many countries, the people have no legal system for investing in a business or private land in their local economy as individuals free from government interference.

I support Mr. De Soto's estimate of approximately $10 trillion dollars of equity in the assets held by citizens in the emerging economies.

There are millions of asset holders that will invest in the new economy and become home buyers. Under new property laws, they could prove ownership of assets and borrow against their equity or sell a portion of their assets to invest in a new home. Under a better system of property rights, many would be able to sell their existing home or use the equity to collateralize a new loan for a new home without selling.

Based on the research completed by De Soto and his associates, he also can show how the value of the savings among the poor is many times larger than the foreign aid they have received for years.

The home building process would begin by qualifying the more affluent and constructing a fully modernized new home in new communities that are fully integrated with commercial, retail and educational facilities.

I have watched my more affluent friends in emerging economies invest in stocks in foreign countries because there were no opportunities for investing in their local economy. Even the private retirement funds managed for citizens in some emerging economies invest in foreign countries in an effort to maximize the return on the behalf of the contributors.

These funds could be utilized in the financing and establishment of a home building industry if the proper laws were in place and experienced management was given the responsibility of making mortgage loans. The investment in domestic home mortgages will energize the national economy.

This will bring about new jobs and an increased ability to contribute to pension funds, which will increase the security and viability of the system for all participants.

It is safe to assume that there are at least four billion (4,000,000,000) people currently living in homes that are inadequate. They have no source of safe drinking water connected to the home, no electricity, and no sewer service.

Assuming four people per household, the total number of affordable homes needed today is one billion (1,000,000,000). If there were 20,000,000 homes constructed per year worldwide, it would take fifty years to meet the current needs.

In the meantime, it is expected that there will be an increase in the population of over three billion (3,000,000,000) over the next forty to fifty years Most of this increase will be in developing countries.

This increases the total demand by an additional 750,000,000 homes over the next fifty years to 1,750,000,000 homes. If one-half of this number is constructed over the next fifty years, at the end of 50 years there will still be 3 billion people without adequate housing.

Considering the fact that the number constructed annually will begin slowly and increase as a function of the ability of the newly employed to qualify, it is difficult to project when the total needs of the next fifty years will be met.

In the United States, the average number of homes constructed is approximately 1,000,000 per year during a boom cycle; although there are times when it is much higher.

The impact on the United States economy from constructing these homes is well known. Imagine constructing at least ten to thirty times that many homes worldwide each year for seventy-five years. That would solve the employment problem for many years.

4. **Quality Housing Creates Moving Up Effect.** In a home building economy, the economic phenomenon known as "moving up" is a principle that is never discussed in economic theories nor is it well understood; however, it has an incredible impact on the lower income groups. Home buyers moving up to a new home increases the prosperity of the lower income groups as they are able to purchase the vacated home and become homeowners.

When 1,000,000 new homes are purchased and the new quali-fied borrowers move in, they will sell or rent their 1,000,000 homes or apartments that have been vacated. This process creates vacancies that were not available to the next lower income group prior to the sale of the new homes. This gives the people in the next lower level of income the opportunity to move up in the quality and size of their homes.

As the second group of vacated units is absorbed, the new resi-dents leave behind lower quality home or rental unit which becomes available to the next lower income group.

This phenomenon is actually measurable in home building econo-mies. The number of existing homes that are sold each year in the United States average three times the number of new homes sold.

Should a country construct and sell 1,000,000 new homes, there would be an additional three million families that would be "mov-ing up" to better housing. Many of those that are on the bottom end of this income distribution spectrum are buying their first home, referred to as "entry level" housing. Just entering the home buying market for the first time, they are qualifying to buy an older, fully improved and standard size home because of a better job. Perhaps some of the jobs were created by the construction of the new homes.

This domino effect will be true of any nation once the process begins to increase employment and wages. This process makes homes at the bottom of the economic scale available to those moving into a home for the first time. It increases the number of quality homes in every city eliminating the need to construct "affordable" housing of little value and limited life.

5. Owning an Appreciating Asset Increases Net Worth. How do we create prosperous nations in emerging economies?

Establish a home building industry. The process will create pros-perity for all people in nations whose laws include protected private property rights.

The legal provisions must provide people the right and the opportunity to borrow the necessary funds to leverage their purchase of an appreciating asset, a home. The home appreciates and increases in value over time as the former rent payments become the source of funds being spent, sometimes by more than one family, to reduce the principal of the debt, thus increasing the net worth of the homeowner. It is, in essence, a forced savings program that increases the sense of security. It is the willingness of those with credit to take risks on home ownership that energizes every successful economy.

The most important characteristic of the process is that the money being borrowed from a bank is only for the specific purpose of buying an appreciating asset. The borrowed funds are based on appraisals and spent only for acquiring products and services needed for the construction of a modern home and a share of public services.

Money spent by governments, corporations, or by the people for any other types of products or services will not increase anyone's net worth. Increasing net worth of working people through the ownership of an appreciating asset is the essential requirement for any nation to become prosperous.

If you are reading about home ownership for the first time, depending on what country you live in, you should know that owning a home will increase your net worth over time as the home increases in value and the debt is reduced. This is the norm when homes are constructed as part of a planned community.

Owning a home creates family wealth and national prosperity. When consumer products for the home are purchased at retail prices, the value of the product drops immediately upon purchase. There is little demand for used items and no opportunity to sell at a higher price. The opposite is true when you purchase private property.

The value of the land and home appreciates over time mostly due to inflation. However, if properly located and constructed, it will improve in value as the demand for housing increases.

Not only is the investment in the home protected by the demand for housing, the amount of the invested equity grows over time as the value of the home increases and the principle amount of the loan decreases. This process permits the homeowner to spend money that would have gone for rent, to reduce the debt and accrue their invested equity. This is what creates a growing net worth for lower income families. In most cases, this is their only way to create net worth.

6. **Insured Mortgages Increases The Number of Borrowers.** An important financing principle requires the incorporation of mortgage insurance and reinsurance of the mortgages into the lending process for developing economies. Mortgage insurance dramatically increases the number of potential lower income buyers that can qualify. It lowers the interest rate on the loan to the lowest achievable rate. Lowering the interest rate is the first objective for the success of this plan.

The lower income groups that will then be able to qualify are the largest and have the greatest need.

By this procedure international financial institutions are protected when extending credit to a subsidiary or a domestically owned bank in emerging economies.

These lenders can rely on the loan being backed by specific loan values based on appraisals provided by the domestic banks.

For emerging economies that may wish to establish domestic mortgage insurance companies, it is critical that the managing agency not be backed or managed by any government. A board consisting of individuals from the real estate industry should be placed in charge of managing the degree and frequency of mortgage insurance. Since the availability of mortgage insurance is one of the most important tools that regulate the lending process, it must not become politicized. Some mortgage insurance companies in the United States are already insuring mortgages in other countries for international lenders.

7. **Guaranteed Title Establishes Legal Ownership.** The establishment, public acknowledgement, and recording of the legal descriptions for private property are fundamental requirements for private property ownership and transfer of land. In some countries, this will require the establishment of title companies that manage the

legal descriptions for the land for the first time. There is now a very practical and precise engineering process made possible by the various Global Positioning Systems (GPS) currently available. Once any specific point is selected as the base line measurements of property, boundaries can be taken utilizing standard engineering procedures and checked by additional GPS readings. When land that was formerly held by a government or large tract owner is sold for the development of homes and communities, the seller must provide proof of ownership and the right to sell.

By establishing a complete title management program for each country, there will be an opportunity for more affluence and therefore more investments in real estate development companies, title companies, and mortgage companies rather than investing in foreign markets.

Initially, in some countries, foreign companies will have the opportunity to step up from domestic investor groups and companies to create new real estate entities for the management of the development process.

In most countries there exist sufficient capital for the establishment and operation of these new companies. Joint ventures will undoubtedly emerge between domestic and foreign investors. Long term foreign ownership will be determined by local laws that will be needed as the economies begin to expand.

8. **Quality Construction Creates Educated and Trained Workers.** The construction of homes for the employed, whether they are teachers, policemen, government workers, or any other affluent group increases the number of people to be educated and trained on the job. The eradication of severe poverty depends on providing education and training in the real estate disciplines including construction, engineering, legal title, escrows, designs, appraisals, financing, and banking. Education, coupled with the creation of jobs, is the strength of this plan which has been proven successful in prosperous nations. Developers constructing homes will be able to invite members of

other countries to participate in this training. In turn, they take their education and experience home to manage their own program.

9. **Newly Employed Become Qualified Buyers.** The newly employed that are receiving on-the-job-training in real estate disciplines become qualified for buying a new home or one of the homes vacated by others moving up. This increases the number of homes to be constructed and increases again the number employed who can afford a new home. New employment expands the demand for consumer services and products domestically and globally as the increased income passes through the hands of the people. The home loans are actually funding manufacturing through the creation of consumer demand. This is what creates prosperity.

10. **Demand for Consumer Product-Increases Global Employment.** Increased employment in the home building industry provides income for people to increase their aggregate demand for consumer products. This is what creates prosperous nations. As the capital is expended for the land, construction of the buildings, acquisition of equipment and labor is released into the economy, it passes through the hands of the people; as they in turn spend, the funds turn over and over, creating a demand for consumer products and services many times greater than the original cost of the home, even after paying taxes on each turn over. The manufactures in emerging economies will have to expand and new companies formed to provide for the refrigerators, heaters, air conditioners, furniture, and clothing, in addition to the construction materials.

As the economy begins to expand in the emerging economies, the demand for skilled and educated people to work will increase in other countries as well. A housing industry creates demand for products and services, many of which will not be initially available domestically. They will have to be imported, which impacts the economies of other nations. The demand created by initially expending billions and eventually trillions of dollars annually in a home building industry for emerging economies will succeed in creating prosperity and energizing the global economy where aid in equivalent amounts has consistently failed. Empirical evidence shows that when housing construction is booming in the United States, imports also increase drastically. When housing construction slows in the United States, the economies of other countries are impacted.

11. **Home Equity Enables Small Business Loans.** The increase in the value of the equity invested in the purchase of an appreciating asset such as a home or a parcel of land over time becomes the predominate source of collateral for personal loans. The equity in personal assets allows people to borrow funds to finance the operation of privately owned small businesses.

Small businesses are the principal employers in prosperous countries when the economy is based on protected private property rights. In countries where protected private property rights exist, well over 66% of the employed work for small businesses either directly or indirectly. Home equity loans are the critical component for increasing the number of small businesses that are the driving force of every national economy where the people are truly prosperous.

If a home goes up 10% in value over 18 to 24 months after purchase, the equity invested by the new homeowner of 10% of the original value doubles. In the United States, the increase in equity is the predominate source of collateral used by homeowners to borrow money for forming a new business.

This has a major impact on the economy of the nation. It is one of principle reasons there are so many successful small businesses that continue to provide a large portion of the employment base.

About half of all private sector workers are employed in small business. Of these, over 10.3 million workers are self-employed. The total work force is approximately 153 million.

12. **Taxes on Loans Used For Infrastructure.** Taxing the home building industry strengthens the viability of governments for the payment of loans whose funding provides for the construction of infrastructure, medical facilities and schools. These support the needs of the people throughout all sections of a city.

The increase in taxes also provides the capital for the repayment of loans borrowed for construction of facilities for the services and infrastructure needed for the specific home building community such as streets, waste disposal and water treatment.

The home building process also includes fees to be paid to governments on the construction of each new home.

These contribute to a fund to pay the new homeowner's share of the cost to extend and provide utilities and roads to each home. In a mathematical model of the various forms of taxation which includes all sales tax, income tax, and government fees charged at every level, the governments will receive 100% of the mortgage funds expended for development and construction of the homes over a period of eight to ten years as the home loan proceeds move through the economy and are taxed at each turn over.

HOW DO DEVELOPED COUNTRIES BENEFIT

A rapid expansion of economies in many countries will require an influx of educated and experienced workers in all aspects of the economy to manage and assist in the development of the impoverished who will become employed.

There will be a tremendous demand for people to travel and perhaps move to the underdeveloped countries to educate the new work force in basic educational skills for real estate development. Opportunities will be created in a wide range of business that will be forming such as restaurants, medical clinics, hotels, schools, and clothing.

This will require assistance from the more developed countries. The enormous number of jobs being created will establish the participating countries as the place to be for those seeking opportunities to start or be part of a new expanding business. Many of those that have migrated to other countries will return home to become part of the emerging economy as soon as the construction begins on the homes.

Imagine what would happen if the global home building industry was successful in working out a multi-billion dollar housing development program for several countries. Assume that the governments would elect to be participants and agree to meet the conditions of the international financing community for financing one million homes a year. This is approximately how many are constructed in the United States on the average each year.

How many experienced and qualified workers from the more industrialized nations would return home or go to another emerging country to take advantage of a booming economy?

There would be a major shift in employment. Employment opportunities would increase as the total labor supply decreased in the more developed countries. At the same time, consumer demand would jump due to the increase in employment in developing countries.

As each additional country is funded, this condition will have a major effect on manufacturing employment worldwide.

The construction companies, engineers, title management companies, sales organizations, and financing companies will employ people in the emerging economies who will then have funds for basic consumer products for themselves and their homes. This is the emerging consumer demand that will drive the global economy.

HOME BUILDING IMPACTS ALL SECTORS OF RELATED ECONOMIES

The housing boom and home financing are directly responsible for the strong economy of the United States and the creation of its enormous prosperity.

The health of the United States economy has had a large impact on the economies of other countries because of the large number of imports. This fact demonstrates how powerful financing of homes is for improving an economy, if managed properly. The creation of a worldwide housing industry of great magnitude will have this same impact on all economies worldwide. The investment of trillions of dollars in emerging economies will improve other participating economies by creating an enormous demand for consumer goods and services.

Past experiences with Japan, Korea and China have shown that as these economies expanded, the more industrialized economies prospered because the demand for goods and services increased at a faster rate than their domestic production.

Funding home loans for an approved plan of development will place a demand on local suppliers who will initially be limited in their ability to respond.

It is important that the rate of development proceed in an efficient manner thus importing will be necessary.

As the economies begin to prosper, there will be an increased demand for industrial equipment and services. This will enable them to establish manufacturing of all types from food production to medical supplies and medical doctors for their domestic economy.

This process begins to reduce the disparity between countries as their cost of goods begins to increase as a product of wages begins to increase. This is now being experienced in countries such as China.

The economic crisis in the United States that was created partially by the excessive funding of real estate slowed not only the United States economy; it also contributed to global unemployment. This is empirical evidence of how spending or not spending large sums of money each year for housing has consequences for the global economy.

The office of the Federal Reserve of the United States officially released a statement in July of 2010, warning the world that the United States economy may take five to six years to recover. There was no mention of a plan that would bring about the recovery in that period of time. As conditions continue to decline, there are no new programs being put forth by any country that would increase global employment.

The economy of the Western European Nations is also in trouble. Questions are being raised about the stability of the European currency. The twenty-seven nations in the European Union have not been able to come to any agreements on how to increase employment and energize their economies.

The economic crisis is still increasing on a global scale which will impact all industrial countries. The inability the United States government to reenergize its economy has resulted in increasing unemployment over the past year.

Unfortunately, none of the current plans of the United States government show any promise of improving employment conditions nationally which will continue to affect the global economy as well. The United States needs to create jobs by assisting the businesses in the United States that adopt this plan.

WHO WILL ADOPT PRIVATE PROPERTY RIGHTS

Many people believe the eradication of severe global poverty is impossible to achieve because many of the governments in underdeveloped countries are resistant to any sort of aid that might create an unmanageable debt for the government.

This proposal for a financing program that will eradicate severe poverty will enrich the governments as well as the people without incurring government debt.

A portion of the funds loaned for the construction of the home will be allocated for payment of subdivision improvements. In addition, the funds spent during construction of homes for materials, labor, and appliances turn over many times. They will move through the economy of participating emerging economies and will be taxed.

The taxing authority will then have the means to provide major infrastructures, schools, and hospitals without the government incurring debt.

A home building industry spending trillions of dollars in countries needing housing will result in a dramatic improvement in government services in many countries. This is the incentive for the leaders of underdeveloped countries to participate in the financing program.

Some people believe there is no known plan that addresses all the issues, lack of education, jobs, investment opportunities, and capital. These are the presumed reasons why over half of the population on this planet remains poor.

Some believe that poverty is a cultural mindset. These prejudices cripple efforts to understand the real causes of poverty.

People are confined to a life of poverty because they are prevented from participating in the economic process as borrowers and investors. Borrowing and investing are common practices for free people, corporations, and governments around the world. The debate changes when we recognize and agree that these same rights possessed by the people to borrow capital and to own private property are crucial to the eradication of poverty.

The establishment of a political and economic environment that provides a practical opportunity for people to own appreciating assets such as homes and businesses, eliminates severe poverty, and establishes the plan for solving both social and economic problems.

CAN CORRUPTION BE ELIMINATED

There is a history of corruption that exists in many emerging economies. Often aid and loans have not gone to the right people for the purpose intended.

There are two general types of corruption to be controlled, the improper disbursement of funds and a judicial system that rules in favor of friends. Concerning the former, standard banking and lending practices would be adopted prior to any funding.

The funding process to domestic banks in each country would be established in the same manner that is used in the United States. International funding to domestic banks would be backed by a specific number of loans at specific loan amounts that are in accordance with standards set by international lenders.

All loans would be subject to appraisals. In many countries with newly established protected private property rights, GPS systems would be used to establish a legal based line for properties. Legal descriptions for each parcel would be prepared by title management companies to be established for each country and insured by the local government for the distribution of funds and establishment of property liens. In some countries corrupt courts often rule against those that are in title and award property to those instigating a dispute improperly.

When this has occurred in the past it has been difficult to determine who owns the property. In a number of emerging countries, those in power choose to protect the people's rights to encourage investments. They adopted severe penalties for judges for awarding assets to the wrong people. That has cured the problem. Failure to maintain an honest judicial system will deter international lenders. Their willingness to continue to lend to domestic banks must terminate until such time assurances are forthcoming that the judicial system will act for the protection of all.

Corruption may not be completely eliminated. It still exists in countries with property rights at the present. However, by following a system based on well defined developments backed by specific loans and appraisals, it will be manageable. The proposed plan is not the same as providing loans or aid to governments without any accountability.

Buyers in these countries know what has been paid in the past for homes, and developers and contractors are experiencing actual costs which can be verified. Biding out the land and construction cost, based on what people are willing to be paid for goods and services in each market, makes it possible to determine the true value even in a changing market.

The bidders list must include price catalogues to be maintained on all suppliers of labor, materials, and equipment. Those suppliers attempting to accelerate the normal increases in their prices would be removed from the bidders list.

WHAT COUNTRIES WILL PARTICIPATE

It is difficult to predict an accurate list of countries that have the leadership willing to become qualified participants.

Obviously, there may have to be changes in leadership in some countries before private property rights can be established.

Many of the free countries struggling to increase their prosperity will be candidates. The increase in the number of free countries indicates that men and women in many formerly un-free counties were determined to work to become politically free. They will now have the opportunity to become economically free and prosperous by becoming investors in their own countries if they adopt these principles.

As reported by a former ambassador of the United States, Mark Palmer, in his book *Breaking the Real Axis of Evil*,[viii] the number of free countries increased from forty-three in 1972 to eighty-nine in 2002. The number of Partial Free countries increased from thirty-eight to fifty-six in the same time period.

Countries not free were reduced to forty-seven out of a total of one hundred and ninety-two countries evaluated.

Emerging free countries can establish very prosperous economies by adopting this economic development plan. At this point in time it is very urgent to do so because of the increasing global unemployment and the availability of global capital.

In 2006, I wrote that it was already obvious that investors in the United States and other countries were unable to find viable investment opportunities primarily because earnings on corporate stocks were unattractive and viable real estate opportunities were limited. The reduced earnings by manufacturing corporations were obviously a result of a lower sales volume due to a lack of demand for more consumer products. As a consequence investors were holding back capital while viable investments were being sought. The global aggregate demand for consumer goods has not increased as of this writing.

At the time I thought that a possible investment plan would be to finance housing in emerging economies that were moving toward permitting more freedom for all men and women in their society. It was suggested that the homes would be sold to the working class and affluent families, many of whom live in homes that are not up to the standard they can afford. The limitation to the number of homes was due primarily to the lack of protected private proper rights and viable financing.

HOW IS INFLATION MANAGED

The management of the rate of funding home building in each participating country will be critical to the success of the economic development plan. The rate of development will vary according to the size of the country and the availability of labor and materials.

As construction continues to bid, a careful monitoring of bids as compared to the start up bids of each project will be necessary in order to regulate the rate of construction. Time must be allowed to create more suppliers and train more workers.

Education will be an important factor in maintaining an acceptable rate of inflation. It is expected, however, that there will be a gradual increase in the price of materials and labor over the twenty or thirty years it will take to construct millions of homes.

A critical management requirement is to create confidence in the suppliers and workers that the program is going to be a continuing effort. Once suppliers understand that the money is available and will continue to be forthcoming, they will begin to expand their capability to meet the expected increase in demand. Therefore, it becomes a major requirement of the funding plan to be able to establish a consistent funding pattern and commit to a specific amount over a defined period in any given market. This is one of the management techniques that will reduce cost and inflationary trends.

In implementing the process, it is important to remember that when those who are greedy, incompetent, or poorly informed about how this process must be managed, the working people will suffer because the economy will be thrown into turmoil and working people will become unemployed.

There are specific economic principles that must be understood and followed by those who initiate programs on a national basis. A balance must be maintained between the rate of increase in credit, demand and employment. This balance will also reduce the economic disparity between nations which will lead to more trade.

PART VI

SUSTAINING EMPLOYMENT
IN THE FUTURE

Participatory Economics is the political freedom of the people to participate in the economy of a nation by having the protected legal right to own property, homes and a business, and to act independently in its management and disposition. This is the key to creating jobs now and for the projected increase in population.

THE NEED FOR MORE PRODUCT CONSUMERS

Approximately two billion people of the global population of almost seven billion are in the product consumer class today. Over the past ten years, those consumers have borrowed and spent, driving up sales until they had acquired one of everything they needed, wanted or could afford. The participation of the other four billion people was limited. At least two billion people are not participating at all. As this book was being written, business and economic publications were predicting a further slowdown in the United States economy through 2014. There is concern over total government debt and the potential reduction in the value of the dollar. As their domestic economies are restructured in an attempt to become less dependent on exports to the West, some Asian countries have increased in their national GDP through home construction. They still need more domestic product consumers to sustain a healthy economy. China has a major home building industry working to meet the enormous needs of the people and increase demand for domestically manufactured consumer products.

ECONOMIC FREEDOM CREATES JOBS

When complete participatory economics governs a nation and people feel free to take risks and initiative to invest in the economy, a development plan emerges that establishes a process of investment that creates jobs and national prosperity.

This is the process the home building industry experienced in the United States. Due to annual funding of an increasing number of new insured home mortgages, construction employment was dramatically increased. As a result of increased employment, the aggregate demand for consumer goods achieved a level of consumer demand for domestic and imported goods unheard of in any economic system. This raised the level of employment in the manufacturing and service industries. This continued the process by creating an enormous demand for more housing and more consumer products. This has been the process for economic development for over sixty years, establishing one of the most economically free and prosperous nations on earth. In 2009 *The Economic Freedom of the World was* produced by the Economic Freedom Network. The report measured the degree to which the policies and institutions of countries are supportive of economic freedom and how Economic Freedom has grown in recent years.

SEVEN BILLION NEW PRODUCT CONSUMERS

Construction of a home for every family reduces severe poverty and adds billions of people to the product consumer class in nations worldwide. Permitting people to invest in the economy through home ownership is a strategy which will increase the number of product consumers by over four billion people. It will increase the global demand for all types of manufactured products, energize the global economy, and create hope in the hearts of the impoverished.

The United Nations reports that over the next forty to fifty years there will be an increase of an additional three billion people, bringing the total population to almost ten billion. It is projected that the increase will take place mostly in the less developed economies. This would increase potential new product consumers to seven billion in less than fifty years. The increase is over three times the number of product consumers sustaining manufacturing now. A global home building industry is the only solution to this pending disaster. Creating that many new buyers for consumer products through home financing must become the number one priority of any nation or business interested in reenergizing and increasing its manufacturing capacity.

More importantly, world peace is achievable for the first time in the history of this planet if prosperity is within the reach of all people. People who are able to purchase personal assets and begin to become prosperous have a major incentive to resolve disputes and forgive grievances. Understanding that there is a way to create global prosperity creates a sense of opportunity which will instill hope in billions of people. As prosperity reduces the disparity of incomes in and between countries, it reduces the tensions that now exist between nations and people. The insane arguments advanced by those who persist in terror against civilians and who desire war for personal or national gain then become untenable by the vast majority of the people now living in poverty.

Up until now, the unanswered question has been how to create jobs that will raise income levels and establish six-billion new product consumers. The history of the most prosperous economy in the world provides the answer.

Jobs created in the home construction industry in the United States raised the standard of living and increased the number of buyers of manufactured products. The solution to creating jobs in global manufacturing is an expanding international home construction industry that is planned and financed for construction homes for almost six billion people over the next forty years. This makes possible a new manufacturing boom using an entirely new type of international financing. It is based on insured mortgage financing of homes to create enormous consumer demands.

SEVEN BILLION NEW TAXPAYERS

The global economic development plan, Participatory Economics, permits people to borrow money to invest in a home which is an asset that appreciates over time. This process energizes economies for a number of reasons. The insured funds are loaned based on viable credit of the people, not the government. The major portion of funds disbursed is for the wages of on-site home construction workers and those who produce the products and materials needed for home building.

The money spent on homes turns over in the economy eight to ten times to energize the economy. By this process, one hundred per cent of the funds is converted to taxes and spent again by governments. It is critical to remember that at each turnover of funds, governments tax the process and use the revenue to provide services without incurring debt.

The magnitude of taxes collected as a result of building homes for seven billion impoverished families completely changes the economics of globalization by strengthening participating governments.

A global home building industry will employ hundreds of millions of workers directly and indirectly as the money circulates around the world. Governments in emerging economies will be able to collect taxes from seven billion new taxpayers over the next thirty years. The power of these economic development principles will be undeniable once a few countries decide to energize their economies by letting their people own private property, borrow money to buy homes, and invest in businesses that support the home building industry.

Governments of participating countries will have the opportunity to magnify the impact they have on poverty by contributing to an established Mortgage Collateral Fund (MCF). A government contribution to the MCF increases the flow of taxable money into the economy by a factor of at least twenty times the amount contributed by the government. This fundamental principle, when adopted by governments, establishes a flow of mortgage funds through an emerging economy while greatly increasing tax revenue. The taxing authorities will eventually possess over seventy-five percent of the loan amounts funded by banks as they tax each turnover of the funds and property acquired. This dramatically increases the strength of governments and improves their ability to provide services to the people.

FREE TRADE BECOMES VIABLE

When participatory economics, is put into practice, the controversy about free trade is reduced. Emerging countries participating in a global home building industry will begin to develop prosperous economies based on increased employment and domestic spending.

For example, employment in home construction creates economic conditions that make mechanized farming affordable and practical.

However, the number of people employed in agriculture raises the standard of living of the entire country only when they can find jobs in urban environments. Fewer people raising the same amount of produce and crops can be paid higher wages. It also lessens dependence on agricultural trade in emerging countries because crops can be sold domestically. Further, it alters the entire purpose for attempting to establish free-trade as it relates to farming.

A home building industry energizes the domestic economy and provides jobs for those no longer working on farms. Funding new manufacturing in emerging countries, in response to increased demand for consumer products creates additional jobs for those migrating to the cities. This substantially reduces many of the problems of emerging economies often associated with international trade. It establishes a stronger economy based on the manufacture of products needed for home construction domestically, one that is less dependent on the international marketplace.

China is an example of how the leaders of an emerging nation have changed their laws. They recognized the need to establish an economic system that permits private property ownership for all. As recently as March of 2007, the leadership of China presented to the National People's Congress a revolutionary new legislation to strengthen the private property rights that were in effect. The bill enforces the right of the people to own private property by stressing the need to protect those rights. This action demonstrates China's continuing commitment to change to a market economy.

It is a step in the right direction. Property rights however, are not being protected sufficiently from corruption.

This lack of law enforcement discourages international financing of home construction. Should China succeed in strict enforcement, there could be a rapid increase in their GDP per capita, if the concept of an International Mortgage Insurance is adopted. It would not be unreasonable for China to construct ten million new homes per year with a population that is almost five times that of the United States; even this would not catch up with the growing demand. China has now created a construction industry based on home construction that could eventually require international financing in the range of $2 trillion dollars per year. A construction program of this magnitude would dramatically reduce the growing economic disparity within China.

The tremendous economic growth China has achieved in recent years is an example to the world of how to increase the prosperity of any country. It is a warning to the leaders of developing economies who continue to restrict private property rights. Their success provides additional empirical evidence of the success of free market principles. Those that choose to ignore the success of countries that have adopted private property rights are doing so for personal gain. China has used the profits from its exports to finance the construction of homes, offices, and infrastructure.

This adds to the strength of its employment base. This has produced a dramatically high annual rate of increase in GDP over the past ten years.

Their GDP growth averaged well over nine percent per year for many years while maintaining a relatively low rate of inflation.

Their domestic economy grew more robust, even as its export economy declined due to construction.

Considering the magnitude of the past annual increases in GDP per capita, shifting the foundation of the Chinese economy has been an extraordinary management accomplishment for an emerging nation.

A GLOBAL PRIORITY

In the past, eradicating global poverty has been an unachievable task. All the agencies, international organizations, governments, and foundations have been working on their own plan without the benefit of a plan that changes the basic economic structure of the countries. Prior splintered efforts have had no single economic development plan that explained the principles to be adopted that are necessary to create prosperity. Past efforts of dedicated and hard-working people made little or no progress because there was no plan for engaging experienced men and women from the business and financial community in one joint effort. The principles of participatory economics are accepted as the rules that create prosperity. This plan makes it possible to bring all interested parties together playing their selected role in a single effort to eradicate severe poverty.

It is time to develop International Mortgage Insurance Agencies to insure homes in the emerging economies.

The adoption and expansion of an insured mortgage lending program for a global home building industry will accelerate the eradication of severe poverty. Global prosperity becomes possible when governments, banks, private investors, NGOs, foundations, corporations, and international agencies agree to support home building as the correct vehicle for creating jobs in the 21st century. Billions of people are waiting.

PART VII

PARTICIPATORY ECONOMICS
THE BASIS OF ECONOMIC FREEDOM

"It is also incumbent on everyone who holds a high governmental office to make absolutely sure that the private property of all citizens is safeguarded, and that the state does not encroach on these rights in any way whatever."

Marcus Tullius Cicero
Roman Statesman,
Philosopher 106-43 BC

A NEW GLOBAL ECONOMIC PARADIGM

The international adoption of Participatory Economics as the principles to be enjoyed by all people will free people and establish a global development paradigm for the 21st century. It will establish the right of all people to become participants in the growth of their country, as investors in their future. It develops prosperity by allowing people to be the main source of credit and providing them with a method of building an estate through the ownership of an appreciating asset.

No one has summarized this powerful truth more clearly, persuasively, and eloquently than journalist Tom Bethell in his book *The Noblest Triumph*[ix]. In discussing the benefits of a private property system Bethell writes,

"[T]here are four great blessings that cannot easily be realized in a society that lacks the secure, decentralized private ownership of goods. These are: liberty, justice, peace and prosperity....Of these, the relationship between liberty and property are now fairly well understood. Leon Trotsky [Russian revolutionary] long ago pointed out that...where there is no private ownership; individuals can be bent to the will of the state, under threat of starvation."

Any time a government pretending to govern in the interest of the people seizes financial institutions or businesses, it runs counter to basic economic principles for solving the problems of an economy. Their true purpose is to increase the power of the governing group and their

ability to manipulate the movement of money into their
own pockets.

Reducing the ability of the government to tax and interfere in
operation of daily business is the right attitude for making change if
the true purpose is to energize an economy and increase prosperity of
the people.

Elite governing classes in many countries today deprive their people of the right to own private property and businesses as a means of
controlling, manipulating, and limiting their economic growth. Global poverty exists due to inhumane limitations imposed by those who
wish to restrict personal property ownership to a select few. Bethell
presents a number of historic illustrations of the benefits of private
property rights for all.

"...like all genuine rights, protect the weak against the strong.
Some early arrivals in the United States marveled that smallholders
were as secure in their possession as the rich were in theirs. A group
of German settlers in Maryland observed in 1763, "The law is so con-
stituted that every man is secure in the enjoyment of his property. [T]
he meanest (poor) person is out of reach of oppression from the most
powerful."

Bethell further states: "The institution of private property also
plays a key role in establishing justice in a society.

This is one of the most important arguments in its favor, yet the
connection between private property and social justice has rarely been
made, mainly because social justice has been equated with the distribution of already existing goods. Inequality is equated with injustice.

Nonetheless, a private property regime makes people responsible
for their own actions in the realm of material goods. Such a system
therefore ensures that people experience the consequences of their
own acts.

Property is also the most peaceable of institutions. In a society
of private property, goods must be either voluntarily exchanged or
laboriously created. As long as such ownership is protected by the

state, goods cannot easily be taken by force. Prosperity and property are intimately connected. Exchange is the basic market activity, and when goods are not individually owned, they cannot easily be exchanged. Free market economies, therefore, can only be built on a private property base."

A KING BESTOWED
PRIVATE PROPERTY RIGHTS

The advent of private property in America came about with the granting of these rights to the original colonists. It was an incentive for them to work on behalf of the King to colonize the North American continent. Participatory economics became the foundation for prosperity in the colonies. Participatory economics laid the groundwork for what occurred in America more than a century and a half later.

Participatory Economics was an integral part of the concept of Participatory Democracy as established by the Declaration of Independence. Bethell draws on and quotes from the journals of one of the early colonists of Jamestown, Virginia:

> "King James I had recently signed a peace treaty with Spain, and soon thereafter a joint-stock company, called the Virginia Company, was formed in London. In May 1607, three small ships sailed up the James River in what is now Tidewater, Virginia. Of the 104 people who had left London, all but 38 were dead within six months of arriving in Virginia, even though the country was fertile and in many ways hospitable. There were mussels and oysters, turkie nests and many Egges, many fruits, as Strawberries, Mulberries, Raspberries and Fruits unknown; meadows great and large, great store of Deere both Red and Fal-

low. The soil was good and fruitfull. With a modicum of industry, the colonists should have been able to survive satisfactorily.

Over two-thirds of them starved to death. The pattern repeated itself even more horribly two years later during what colonists called "the starving time" of 1609-10. Within six months, the population at Jamestown was reduced from about 500 to 60.

In May 1611, Sir Thomas Dale arrived in Jamestown as high marshal. Dale is credited with instituting a strict penal code and more importantly, private property."

Bethell cites the writings of Jamestown colony secretary Ralph Hamor, which were published in 1615 in England:

"Sir Thomas Dale hath taken a new course throughout the whole colonie...and this it is, he hath allotted to every man in the colonie, three English acres of cleere corne ground, which every man is to mature and tend, being in the nature of farmers...and they are not called unto any service or labour belonging to the Colonie, more than one month in the yeere, which shall neither be in Seed time, or in harvest, for which, doing no other dutie to the Colonie, they are yeerely to pay into the store two barrels and a halfe of Corne." (Hamor, The True Discourse of the Present Estate of Virginia, 1615; original spelling and punctuation)

It is ironic that Participatory economics the underlying principle which makes participatory democracies successful, was not claimed by the colonists at Jamestown, but rather was bestowed upon them by the authority of the Crown, in the person of Sir Thomas Dale. The effects of this were both immediate and, as four centuries of history have demonstrated, critical for the development of a prosperous nation.

"As soon as the colonists were thrown upon their own resources, and each freeman had acquired the right of owning property, the colonists quickly developed what became the distinguishing characteristic of Americans: an aptitude for all kinds of craftsmanship coupled with an innate genius for experimentation and invention." Bethell, The Noblest Triumph)

What caused such a remarkable change in the work ethic of the settlers?

The principle of private property ownership energized the colonials. Owning property does more than just impose a direct responsibility for oneself and family on the individual. It instills an even greater sense of opportunity to succeed. Ownership naturally changes the mores and morals of a society. These changes have proven impossible for tyrannical governments to accomplish. More than three centuries after the birth of private property rights in the New World, officials in America, Europe, Asia, and Africa and many others in countries around the globe must learn this lesson.

INDEPENDENCE

Participatory economics defines the economic principles which are the foundation of every successful participatory democracy, where the people elect representatives and where there is direct control of government by the people. The authors of the American Revolution and other colonists who staked their lives in support of the movement to gain independence from England understood this principle. They were business owners, farmers, and professionals who built their livelihoods and raised their families on the firm foundation of secure ownership and protection of private property.

For over one hundred and fifty years, the original colonists experienced prosperity that resulted from exercising their right to own property and businesses.

However, the English rulers excluded the colonists from the decision making process concerning taxation. The elite ruling classes often assumed this as their right.

The King and Parliament levied taxes against privately owned property in the form of goods and services in the colonies without giving them representation in the government process. This was one of the major factors in the colonist's decision to declare their independence. (See the First Addendum)

Through hard work to build a new civilization, the colonists had become very prosperous. History has recorded the astonishment of the King's soldiers when they arrived in America to put down the rebellion. The soldiers were impressed with the prosperity of the farmers and merchants. They could scarcely believe the level of wealth and comfort they enjoyed that they were not free to enjoy in England.

In enumerating his "four great blessings" of secure private property ownership, Tom Bethell might have included a fifth blessing, life itself. His vivid descriptions of the experience of the earliest English settlements in North America illustrate how the introduction of private property rights was a lifesaving phenomenon for colonists in the first decades of 17th century America. This blessing, if granted, could apply to all countries where the lack of private property rights has created extreme poverty and suffering.

FROM KEYNESIAN TO HAYEK ECONOMICS

As the industrial revolution began to expand during the reconstruction of Europe and Japan after World War II, there again rose up economists and political leaders who still believed in socialistic theories that had been tried in the 1930s.

Their school of thought holds that government should play a central role in economic planning and the ownership of industries and land. Economists and other intellectuals in the United States of America had become enthralled with the ideas of John Maynard Keynes in the 1930s under the leadership of President Franklin Roosevelt.

As the worldwide economic Depression of the 1930s deepened, traditional free-market capitalism fell into disfavor in many countries. Government policymakers around the world tried various socialistic remedies in an attempt to fix their shattered economies. The Depression in the United States increased in its severity as socialistic theories were implemented in an attempt to energize the economy.

Economic planning by governments and government ownership of industries began to expand and take hold in a number of countries. After years of trial and error, long after the Depression ended, many came to believe the various socialistic approaches to economic development had failed. The free market doctrines of Friedrich von Hayek advanced as early as the mid 1940s did not begin to find acceptance in Britain until the early 1970s.

Lectures and writings of Von Hayek's disciple, American Milton Friedman also began accelerating interest in free-market principles in the United States.

Daniel Yergin and Joseph Stanislaw, in their book *The Commanding Heights*[x], chronicled the transition from the Keynesian economy and welfare-oriented forms of capitalism to the free-market system advocated by Friedrick Hayek. The book is a history of the changes in global thinking that laid the foundation for the adoption of free-market principles by emerging economies.

Over the past sixty years, this change in thinking has been a general awakening among the leaders of emerging economies. Yergin and Stanislaw point out how countries such as China came to realize that centralized planning and government ownership of banks and companies has proven not only to retard economic development; it created shortages and added to the poverty of many countries. Government ownership of manufacturing facilities has failed to provide the goods society needs. In most cases, such government-owned corporations operated at a loss, creating an additional burden on the governments.

The data on economically free countries, as measured by the Heritage Foundation's publication, ***Index of Economic Freedom*** (Washington D. C.) provides some insight into the factors that contribute to prosperous countries. Fifty independent variables grouped into ten broad indices score the change in prosperity of 155 countries as they have adopted various portions of the free-market system in recent years. These indicate, to some degree, the direction of change in economic freedom in each country from year to year.

Those countries where private property is limited or does not exist are not keeping up with the rapid growth of the more economically free nations. However, the report fails to mention the degree to which private property ownership exists. One of the most important indices of economic freedom is the number of homes per capita and percentage of homes privately owned. Without this knowledge, it is impossible to accurately measure the degree to which economic freedom truly exists.

The disparity between the GDP per capita of the most and least economically free countries is substantial.

Despite the efforts of international agencies and governments to provide billions of dollars in foreign aid and financing for economic development in under developed countries poverty is increasing Attempts have been made to establish an economic development strategy focused on increasing the manufacturing capability of developing nations for the purpose of increasing exports. This method relies on the hope that creating more manufacturing jobs will strengthen a nation's economy. Unfortunately, statistics show that increasing employment in manufacturing has not increased prosperity appreciably for the vast majority of people in developing nations.

Low-wage employment in manufacturing, spurred by government aid and loan programs, has not and cannot create the tremendous prosperity that is possible by correctly applying all of the free-market principles defined by participatory economics.

The prosperity that flows from participatory economics is available to all people in any country. It was not growth in low wage employment that brought prosperity to millions of Americans after World War II. The creation of millions of jobs was the direct result of initiating a home building industry based on the idea of constructing large subdivisions.

CREATING PROSPEROUS GOVERNMENTS

No nation can rise economically above the prosperity of its people without Participatory Economics. To understand how poverty can be eradicated, it is important to recognize how the economic principles described above work in prosperous countries to create viable governments where millions of people have achieved high levels of prosperity.

The degree to which a government can become financially healthy by taxing the prosperity of the people determines the wealth of a nation. If the men and women are not prosperous, no government is capable of meeting the needs of the people, including providing national security without sacrificing natural resources. This becomes obvious when countries managed by tyrants use their meager resources for a military buildup. It relegates the people to poverty, poor health services, and minimal education. Many people in this environment do not realize that they have the intelligence and the ability to reform their economy in a manner that will create prosperity for all.

Even a responsible government is restricted in its efforts to provide for the needs of the people when vast numbers of people pay little or no taxes because they are impoverished. Investing in private property produces a larger tax base with more people paying taxes. It also strengthens the ability of the governments to provide services.

The United States is one example of how a free market economy creates prosperity by the incorporation of the critical principles of participatory economics for all people,

The collected empirical evidence explains what happened in The United States over the past sixty years and illustrates in detail how the structure of state and federal laws encouraged and protected the property rights of each citizen and the right to participate in the process of capitalism.

Understanding how economic freedom was established in the United States is vital to understanding how it was possible for its people to become so enormously prosperous.

Public and private institutions encourage and manage the buying and selling of private property and financing of small businesses. Mortgage insurance, which protects mortgage lenders, encourages the financial community to make loans to people in the lower income levels. This creates a favorable investment opportunity for working people of all eco-nomic levels. Changing global thinking about the economics of property is the key to the eradication of global poverty and the creation of jobs globally in the 21st century.

IMMIGRANTS SUCCEED IN FREE COUNTRIES

Immigrants succeed in free economies. Nowhere are their successes more obvious than in countries where participatory democracy and participatory economics co-exist. In such countries, many immigrants experience economic and political freedom for the first time in their lives. I often heard people comment in emerging economies that even if changes to the political structure could be made and private property rights became law, the economy would not improve for a number of reasons they often quote.

There is no evidence that they are unable to succeed because of personal values, attitudes, or mindsets inherited from their native cultures. On the contrary, there is ample evidence of rapid improvements in personal income and net worth once they understand private property rights.

Immigrants from every continent and culture not only succeed in free economies, they often excel.

In many cases they become more successful than native citizens who do not appreciate the opportunities a free economy offers to all.

Many immigrants will take on more than one job. Most immigrant families have two or more members working. Before long they begin to take risks they would not have attempted in their native land. They begin to borrow money. Soon they own new clothes, a car or truck and a home. Millions of working families have sent money back to their native land amounting to billions of dollars to help those left behind.

Many start their own business and become prosperous without fear of having the business taken from them, which would not have been possible for many of them in their native culture. In general, people do not have a mindset that prevents them from becoming prosperous. Rather, their natural mindset includes a willingness and determination to work and achieve a better life that becomes obvious, no matter what country or culture they come from. When they exercise that natural right and act on the opportunity to participate in a free economy as investors as well as workers, they work very hard to become wealthy.

There is ample evidence that once nations pass private property rights laws, the people will eagerly take up their new freedom to invest in their own economies and become prosperous.

When these men and women come to understand what is possible with the passage of protected private property rights, they can join this movement organized to help them become economically free.

After learning of this plan, they also come to realize with private property rights laws in place, there will be companies and financial institutions who are willing to assist them, to build homes, should they decide to act.

GOVERNMENT SERVICES

Governments benefit from the implementation of participatory economics because the construction, sale, and furnishing of a home involve numerous taxable transactions. It begins with the harvesting, processing, manufacturing and sale of building materials and continues through the manufacture, sale, installation, and service of mechanical equipment and appliances and everything else that goes into a new home.

Taxes are collected from every person and business involved in this process. By the time the money from home mortgages is spent and re-spent it turns over eight or nine times as it passes through the economy. Meanwhile the governments collect taxes that total more nearly 100% of the initial cost of a home over an eight to ten year period, depending on local tax rates.

Essentially, the homeowner borrows funds for home construction that also energizes an economy and becomes the source of much of the government funding needed for providing services.

As a nation's GDP increases, tax revenues increase as well. This provides money for defense, health care, education and improved public infrastructure without governments incurring large debts.

Taxing economic activity is unquestionably the most effective method governments can use to generate the funds needed to provide services, the expenditure of which further enhances the economy.

DOMESTIC CONSUMPTION

To understand how prosperity feeds upon itself, first it is critical to recognize that money borrowed for home construction and buying a home is different from foreign aid or short-term bank loans to governments and manufacturing corporations. The most important difference is that the people use the money to buy appreciating assets, which increase in value over time thereby providing a method for even the lowest wage earner to develop net worth.

Second, repayment is the responsibility of the people. Third, there is the impact on the economy as the money spent for labor and materials passes from one person to another, each purchasing good and services that create a demand for a wide variety of consumer products. The need for labor and materials to build a home creates the initial jobs.

The continuing turnover of the money rolling through the economy each year as more homes are constructed creates more jobs in other industries and other countries, further expanding the nation's domestic and global economy.

In contrast, the expenditure of limited wages by the people for consumer products does not create prosperity. It is the leveraging of a small portion of the limited wages for the purpose of repaying long term loans which finances the economy on a major scale.

BUYING AND SELLING HOMES

As the incomes of the owners increase over time, they sell their homes to take advantage of the increase in their equity to make a down payment on a larger home.

In the United States, homeowners are constantly selling their homes and moving up to larger homes. Approximately every five to seven years they sell and use the increased equity to purchase another home, thereby leveraging their income again, perhaps with a larger debt. This process places existing homes back on the market. The number of existing homes that sell each year is often three times or more the number of new newly constructed homes sold in the United States. Many sales require the buyer to increase the existing mortgage amount, which invests more new capital into the economy and increases the impact of home ownership. Millions of Americans have established relatively large financial estates by paying off their mortgage debt over time.

A HOME BUILDING ECONOMY

The principles of participatory economics succeed when a government creates a political and economic environment that provides its entire population, including the poorest of working families, the protected right and means to acquire private property, homes, and businesses through practical mortgage financing. It is this process that enables a country to launch a national construction and investment industry that increases employment and prosperity. The increase in employment establishes a continually growing class of prosperous investors, homebuyers, product consumers, and taxpayers.

If it is true that prosperity in any country can be created by permitting all people to be personally and substantially involved in the economic development process, a question arises:

How is individual economic involvement possible in an underdeveloped country where so many people are unemployed and living in poverty? The answer is that the loans are initially made to those with some income or net worth and established credit so they can obtain better housing. Initially large and medium size homes will be constructed in accordance with the net worth of the upper and middle income group. This begins the process.

Prior attempts to begin a home building industry by building initially for the lowest income groups have failed. This approach will always require that the sponsoring government subsidize the rents or mortgage payments. Because of the large percentage of the subsidy required, governments are limited in the number that can be constructed. As a consequence, only a very minimum number of jobs are established and when unemployment becomes a problem, the homes are vacated as the workers seek employment in other cities.

It has been found that in most underdeveloped countries those in the upper income levels live in homes that are below a standard of quality and size that they could afford if financing was available.

Many are restricted to renting even when they have the funds and the credit to purchase a home. Selling homes to those who have funds or credit establishes new construction jobs for the unemployed who then become qualified to borrow for the purpose of purchasing their own home.

Initially the process is gradual; however, it has been proven that it spreads very rapidly as those who are now working to manufacture materials and furnishings for homes. They also become qualified to purchase a new home.

ATTRIBUTES OF A CONSTRUCTION ECONOMY

Here are some attributes of private property economies that permit the lending of money to build homes.

ESTABLISHING FAMILY CREDIT

Several methods are used to verify the small amount of net earnings that the working poor are able to save at the end of each month. It is possible to verify employment, tax payments and cash savings to name a few. The verification of net earnings establishes the amount of credit needed to qualify as a borrower to buy a home. Establishing a credit bureau is the first step in making it possible for the working families to spend future earnings in the present.

DOMESTIC ENTREPRENEURS

A new national home building industry provides investment opportunities for domestic investors in participating countries and international investors to sponsor the construction of subdivisions and the sale of homes. The opportunity to invest in local businesses does not exist in many countries because of the lack of private property rights. The expansion of home construction in turn increases the need for investors to sponsor domestic manufacturing of materials, equipment, and appliances, along with home furnishings.

This results in an increase in employment globally as hundreds of millions of homes are constructed in each country. Providing a safe and viable investment for domestic capital also reduces the amount of capital that leaves the country to be invested internationally.

INCREASING NET WORTH

There is a worldwide belief, especially by people in emerging countries, that in times of unbridled inflation it is disastrous to hold savings in cash or in a bank. They understand the principle reason for home ownership. Over time a home increases in value, particularly during times of inflation, and protects their cash invested. Owning a home provides a means to protect any net earnings invested in the home that is not required for daily living. The monthly mortgage payment reduces the debt on the home. This process increases the net worth of families who own homes.

MANUFACTURING JOBS

As millions of new homes are sold to working people, millions of new construction jobs are created.

The industries that are required for the private property system to function include mortgage lenders, title and escrow companies, real estate sales offices, and manufacturing companies to provide all of the materials, carpets, tile, and appliances.

Typically, many of these jobs pay well above the minimum wage. The establishment of construction jobs develops the large middle class that is missing in so many countries.

The unemployed and impoverished become employed and eligible to buy homes. This is how to help the poor.

Welfare, in the form of free education, medical attention, or direct payments, does not permit people to enter into a personal process of generating wealth.

REDUCING GOVERNMENT DEBT

Governments become financially strong where there is a viable home building industry supported by insured mortgages. Prosperity increases the stability of the economy and the borrowing capacity of businesses.

Money initially spent to buy a home is taxed at least eight times as it moves through the economy before its buying energy is depleted. Increasing tax revenue enables governments to more effectively meet the needs of the people and provides money to reduce public debt. The reduction of public debt stabilizes the government and the economy. Governments unencumbered by foreign debt have more flexibility to adjust taxes if necessary to stimulate the economy.

STRENGTHENING DOMESTIC BANKS

Funds borrowed by banks participating in the International Mortgage Insurance Agency's program are loaned to homeowners for payment to contractors and suppliers. These funds strengthen the viability of domestic banks as hundreds of millions of dollars flow through the system. This energizes the economy at a level that welfare and minimum wage jobs cannot possibly achieve. The establishment of insured mortgages gives banks the ability to sell mortgages domestically and internationally to replenish capital loaned to homebuyers through the securitization of the mortgages.

An energized economy based on the construction and sale of homes requires the expansion of professional banking services to monitor the lending process. Ensuring that the funds from the international banking community are used efficiently in the construction of homes is the responsibility of the participating banks. Their success as the manager of the process determines the willingness of the international banking community to continue to commit funds.

INFRASTRUCTURE COST

A portion of the money borrowed for each new home provides an additional source of revenue to governments in the form of impact fees for the construction of water and waste treatment facilities, energy generation and distribution, schools, hospitals, and roads. Absorbing a small portion of the cost of the infrastructure by the mortgage loan to be repaid by the homeowner over thirty years further enhances the government service.

HOME OWNERSHIP CHANGES CULTURAL BELIEFS

Men and women everywhere will always work to create prosperous conditions when permitted and encouraged to participate in the economy of a country governed by a true form of anticipatory democracy. In countries around the world, people prosper or struggle to the degree that governments protect their personal and economic freedoms. The freedom to engage in the economic process is what changes and energizes people's outlook when they become borrowers and investors.

The attributes of a culture related to agriculture, seaports, or climates does not determine whether or not people will make the effort to become prosperous. Cultures develop over time because of economic and political conditions, which determine how people think about themselves and their place in society. People behave as they do because of their belief or lack of belief in the possibility of achieving their goals.

All people instinctively want to be prosperous and healthy. However, when governmental restrictions and the lack of economic freedom, are a fact of life they become discouraged and depressed.

They lose hope because of the lack of opportunity. They learn ways that help them to cope. They become conditioned to failure. They are forced to adopt limited goals, which in turn reduce their motivation to succeed. Many withdraw from society into family groups in an effort to survive. Others turn to crime. Cultures develop because of conditions created by economic incentives or lack of incentives; cultures do not create the conditions. It is absurd to believe that religious people are proud of being poor. When allowed to express their feelings, people will make it very clear that they would rather eat well and sleep in a comfortable home than sleep on the ground and go hungry for moral reasons.

A daily struggle just to find food and shelter is a powerful force that undermines the will of the people. People become apathetic when they cannot find any opportunity to improve their family's economic conditions. This leads to estrangement from the rest of society that eventually creates impoverished communities.

The implementation of participatory economics changes this thinking and creates a new culture because the people begin to have hope. When people realize that they can be the driving force of an economy, their natural desires for privacy, safety, and prosperity win out over the myths of ideologies and ancient cultures. Progressive cultures are the byproduct of people exercising personal freedom, both political and economic.

Study participatory economics and come to know that there is a viable economic development plan. Get involved in creating a global network of those concerned and dedicated to spreading the word.

The Fourth Addendum entitled "What You Can Do" explains how you can help men and women in countries around the world achieve economic freedom and prosperity. Use your passion. Take action to create jobs! Stop millions of lives being lost each year because of starvation and disease.

To help you in this effort, you can order copies of this book on Amazon and give them to those who have the desire to help over four billion men, women, and children living in inhumane environments with no opportunity to find work or adequate shelter and food. Learn what you can do about helping the worldwide plan to create jobs in the 21st century and eradicate severe global poverty.

PART VIII

EMPIRICAL ECONOMIC DATA

Empirical evidence shows that the enormous prosperity of the United States is the direct result of the establishment of a home building industry. It has been the paradigm for global economic development for the past sixty years. It is no long a valid process. Expanding the global home building industry is the correct plan for creating jobs and global prosperity in the future. Statistics show an increase in national and global employment as a direct function of the number of housing starts In the United States. It is imperative that nations adopt this plan to eliminate the suffering from extensive poverty and homelessness in emerging economies.

HOUSING AN ECONOMIC INDICATOR

The direct cause of prosperity in the United States is the economics of home ownership. Economics is often described as a science. But while the so-called "hard" sciences have proofs, theorems, and formulas that consistently and unerringly lead one from A to B, economics has no such mechanism. Bernard Baumohl author of *The Secrets of Economic Indicators*[xi] points this out but also identifies what could be viewed as an exception.

Baumohl writes:

"Looking for a single infallible indicator that can foresee the future direction of the economy? Forget it; you won't find any. However, there is one that comes surprisingly close, and that is housing. Excluding one instance, there has never been a recession in the U.S. at a time when the housing sector stood strong. Only once since the end of World War II did the economy contract despite a robust housing market, and that was in 2001. Even then, the recession was brief and not very deep. This impressive track record is why many experts view home building as one of the most reliable leading indicators of economic activity."

Once we understand how funds from home mortgage loans increase aggregate demand, and aggregate demand increases manufacturing employment, we move closer to understanding how the proposed economic plan has impacted the economy of the United States over the numerous development cycles.

PROSPERITY IN THE U.S.A.

Less than sixty years ago, after struggling through a depression that crippled every economy on earth, and a World War that threatened freedom everywhere, the United States economy began expanding at an unexpected and unprecedented rate. By the passage of a law enabling mortgage insurance to be issued by the Federal Housing Administration (FHA) and the Veterans Administration (VA) to mortgage lenders, an economic development plan was established that permitted Americans in the United States to build the most dynamic and prosperous economy the world had ever seen.

Establishing a method for mortgage insurance companies to provide insurance to lenders and reimburse the lenders in the event of a default by the borrower established an entirely new type of economy. The establishment of government-backed mortgage insurance helped millions of modest-income workers to become homeowners and put tens of millions of people to work. The federal government created a financial environment for private enterprise to launch a home building industry that created millions of jobs throughout the country, thus creating aggregate demand for consumer goods that is the driving force of manufacturing. Home building became, and remains, the primary and most powerful controlling engine that drives the United States economy.

In the recent case where improper lending standards disrupted the U.S. economy, loans were made which were not in accordance to very specific lending and economic guidelines. The health of the nation's economy is directly linked to the health of the home building industry. Today, the economy of United States struggles to recover from ignorant and excessive financing of homes that is now affecting the global economy. Participatory economics is based on increasing aggregate demand by providing a method for loaning money to people for the purchase of a home. This financing process changed the United States from a nation of renters with few private homes in 1940 into a nation of homeowners. It can succeed globally by encouraging the development of international mortgage insurance for home mortgages in developing countries. International Mortgage Insurance encourages the international financing community to make loans to domestic banks in any country that guarantees its men and women the right to own property, and protects those rights by enforcement of the law.

Participatory economics explains how people and institutions in prosperous countries can organize and act to create an opportunity for the people in each developing nation to solve their unemployment problem and establish prosperity. It is an opportunity for help men and women everywhere to secure their inalienable rights, including life, liberty and the pursuit of happiness. This is the basis of natural law that governs the lives of all people in every country.

The opportunity becomes feasible once men and women everywhere understand that it is possible for a nation to become prosperous under this plan.

They must create an environment where the principals of participatory democracy and participatory economics (which are interdependent) are operative. This will free men and women from any form of political or economic enslavement.

PARTICIPATORY ECONOMICS AT THE START

The application of participatory economics has made the United States, from its earliest colonial period, the land of opportunity where people could work and be protected. After the Second World

War prosperity began to accelerate because of home construction. The most dramatic and instructive illustration of this truth came in the first decade after the end of World War II. In the late 1940s and early 1950s, the United States faced a critical shortage of jobs. Poverty was at its highest level since the Great Depression, 1929 to 1940, when nearly one-quarter of the U.S. work force was unemployed.

After World War II, there was a great concern that the shortage of jobs, combined with a shortage of housing and a nearly non-existent home building industry would create an economic crisis similar to the Depression. This is not unlike the problems many countries around the world are currently experiencing. In the 20s and 30s, city populations in the United States were growing rapidly as people moved from farms to urban centers. The work force on America's farms had been dropping steadily, from 40% in the late 1800s to 20% by the 1940s. Today it stands at less than 2%. People leaving farms and migrating to the cities could not find work or places to live.

The same is happening in many countries today. Tractors reduce the need for workers while families on farm grow too large to be supported just by the farm. This has created slums on the outskirts of cities around the world.

In the United States bread lines formed to feed the unemployed. Families were doubling up just to have a place to live. Most of the places they found were less than modest. Homes built in the first half of the 20th century left over 33% of U.S. families without running water. Over 40% of homes did not have indoor toilets.

After World War II, unemployment was again becoming a major economic problem, soon reaching almost 7. %. Men and women released from military service and war-related industries were unable to find jobs. When the war ended, manufacturing began to decline. What is more, manufacturing companies could not justify expanding their payrolls because of the unemployment and lack of demand for consumer products.

A NEED FOR FIVE MILLION HOMES IN 1945

Housing construction during World War II had not kept pace with the needs of the people. Housing starts had declined to approximately 100,000 per year by the end of the 1930s. After the war, housing starts were in the range of 100,000 per year and were not keeping pace with the number of new families created as veterans returned home. The new demand for housing compounded a housing problem that had been growing for more than fifteen years. By the end of 1945, the problem had become a crisis; the United States was in dire need of about five million new homes.

LEVITTOWN STARTED THE HOUSING INDUSTRY

The problem was most severe in the nation's biggest cities, and the solution first took shape just outside the largest city in America. In May of 1947 on Long Island, New York, William Levitt had a dream to create the first modern community for those with modest income just twenty miles from downtown Manhattan. He and his brother Alfred announced plans to build 2,000 mass produced rental homes at Hempstead, Long Island. Two days later, newspapers reported that 1,000 of the homes had already been rented. The community became known as Levittown.

In order to meet that kind of demand, the Levitts made sure their supply of quality building materials was as efficient and inexpensive as possible. All the lumber for the houses was precut and shipped from a California lumber yard the brothers owned, and where they also built a nail factory. Two years after their initial announcement, the Levitts began building "ranch" houses to sell. There were five models and the only differences were in color, roof line, and the placement of the windows. All were built on concrete slabs, had no garage, and came with an attic that could be finished to expand the living space inside the home. They provided the ability to expand the home; this was a stabilizing force for the development of the community. Today it is overlooked by builders of so-called "starter" homes. The public's response was even more enthusiastic than it had been for Levittown rentals. The Levitts came up with an "assembly line" procedure for homebuyers, who could choose the model they wanted and sign a contract for it within three minutes.

Through 1950 and 1951, the Levitts built almost 17,500 homes in Levittown and the surrounding areas. Because of home construction, the local economy was expanding and new homeowners began working at the newly created good-paying jobs as they started their families. Levitt models and the surrounding community were changing to meet the needs of growing families. The ranch style homes built in 1950 came with a carport and a twelve and-a-half inch TV set built into the living room staircase. The 1951 model included a partially finished attic. Shopping centers, playgrounds, and a community center sprang up to meet the demands of Levittown's active families. A magazine devoted to decorating, expanding, and remodeling Levitt homes became almost required reading for Levittown residents. From the beginning, Bill Levitt knew he was building more than just houses. He was building a community, where working Americans of modest means could buy into the "American Dream" and help build what was the most dynamic economy in history. Fast forward to 2005 where Americans built more than 1,850,000 homes in spite of the fact that there were already more than 120 million existing homes built to modern standards in a nation of 300 million people. Constructing an average of over one million new homes per year has become a national standard.

Empirical evidence from the American home building experience that began in the 1940s and 1950s, illustrates the application of an economic development principle that actually increases prosperity for all people, a principle unknown to most economists.

The nation's reaction to a shortage of jobs and a shortage of housing helped launch a major industry that remains today the single most important employer and contributor to the American economy. It created millions of domestic jobs as America became a manufacturing giant and world-wide exporter of consumer products.

Baumhol supports the argument why this continues to be so: "Another critical aspect of the home building industry is how powerful an influence it has on the rest of the economy through what are known as multiplier effects. By multiplier effects, we mean that changes in the pace of housing construction can have major ramifications for many other industries. Just look at who benefits when housing is strong. A jump in residential construction drives up demand for steel, wood, electricity, glass, plastic, wiring, piping, and concrete. The need for skilled construction workers such as bricklayers, carpenters, and electricians soars as well. By one estimate, for every 1,000 single-family homes under construction, some 2,500 full-time jobs and nearly $100-million in wages are generated. A vibrant home-selling market also accelerates the purchase of furniture, carpets, home electronics, and appliances. Housing is thus a major swing industry in the economy because it can affect so many diverse businesses. Home construction became the principle reason Americans were able to lift themselves out of poverty and create a high standard of living. The Federal Government played an essential role in that development by constructing and passing laws that encouraged home ownership."

REMOVE THE BARRIERS TO PROSPERITY

The barrier to the expansion of new home construction centered on the inability of financial institutions to make loans. In addition to the many Americans who were unemployed, many working Americans earned such low wages that they could not qualify under conventional lending requirements. New federal legislation removed that barrier to development by granting the FHA authority to provide mortgage insurance as a protection and an encouragement for the financial community. In 1944, Congress enacted the GI Bill of Rights and expanded the Federal Housing Administration. This gave different agencies of the FGA to guarantee mortgage payments to lenders on behalf of the borrowers. The mortgage insurance also permitted the lowering of interest rates because of the reduced risk to the lenders. The combination of the guarantee and lower interest rates greatly increased the number of potential homebuyers and launched a major housing construction industry that continues today.

The 1,000,000 newly-built homes Americans purchased in the late 1940s sold for an average of $15,000. This released $15 billion into an economy that was struggling because of the lack of employment. It was almost 22% of the total economy. At least 4.5% of GDP of the nation which is currently about $14 trillion still comes from home building alone. In 2005, the construction of over 1.6 million homes, with an average selling price of $250,000, pumped some $400 billion dollars into the economy. The impact of $400 billion dollars on the manufacture and purchase of other products and services is huge. The $400 billion turns over eight or nine times as it moves through the economy. It then becomes obvious that the right to private property and viable mortgage funds are the most important drivers of any industrialized economy.

PROTECTED PRIVATE PROPERTY RIGHTS

Constitutional laws dating back to the founding of the country provided for private property and its protection. The enforcement of the right of ownership made it possible for land and homes to be used as collateral for lenders. People who already owned homes were encouraged to move up to larger homes because they could qualify for higher mortgages, thanks to lower interest rates and the benefits of income tax deductions for interest. The homes they vacated provided housing for the next group. Mortgage insurance guaranteed repayment to lenders in the event of default. That eliminated the barrier which had prevented working families in lower income levels from owning homes. In the early stages, mortgage insurance was critical to the process of making home ownership possible for millions of Americans who would have not qualified under earlier conditions. Over the past 50 years, the importance has declined as the strength of the housing industry and the national economy has reduced the risk of foreclosure.

Millions of jobs in home construction increased the prosperity of the nation as money borrowed for mortgages flowed into the economy. Construction employment produced new consumers and the rising demand for consumer products energized post-war manufacturing as the average income level began to rise. This sequence of events firmly established an economic development system based on a home building industry that tends to stabilize the economy. It has become a driving force in the economy and a significant portion of the GDP for the United States when the impact of the mortgage funds turn over as they pass through the economy.

INCREASING NET WORTH

Remember that money borrowed for the purchase of an appreciating asset impacts the economy in a dramatically different manner than ordinary earned income. Money introduced into the economy through the process of buying a home increases aggregate demand while at the same time converts the rent payment, an expense, to a mortgage payment which increases the equity in the home. This is known as leveraging your income: borrowing a large sum of money to be spent in one year and paid back by monthly payments. Owning an appreciating asset increases the net worth of all homeowners.

New home purchases increase aggregate demand for consumer products dramatically because the money comes from loans to be paid by future income rather than current earnings. Money is spent in one year that will be earned over the next thirty years by millions of people. The money is spent for building materials, large appliances, and construction labor. Money borrowed annually for a home purchase is a multiple of the buyer's current annual income. It multiplies the spending power into millions of dollars when millions of homes are constructed annually, greatly increasing the aggregate demand throughout the global economy each year.

The mortgage insurance concept ushered in a revolutionary reorganization of the economy, but it wasn't part of a grand plan. It was a practical solution to two pressing problems; not enough houses and not enough jobs. However, the advent of mortgage insurance resulted in very favorable unintended consequences.

It launched a new economic development process that became a plan for increasing prosperity by constructing homes for people from all income groups. More importantly, insured mortgages lowered interest rates, which enabled lower income families to invest in their first home. They were encouraged to borrow against the income they would earn in the future and invest those dollars in a home. The equity in their homes grew as they made monthly mortgage payments, and the cost of new homes increased each year. At last, families on the bottom of the economic ladder began to have hope.

Equity in an asset as a relatively small percentage of the total value of a real asset increases rapidly in times of inflation. This increases the total value of the asset.

When the total value of a home goes up because of inflation, the equity becomes a larger percentage of the new value because the larger total value increases while the debt remains fixed or is reduced by payments on the principal.

That's why home ownership increases a family's net worth faster than the rate of inflation. The cost of a new identical home ten years later will obviously be much higher because inflation increases the materials for home construction. This principle is central to understanding how to eradicate severe global poverty.

Manufacturing capacity actually expanded so much that America became a major exporter of consumer products as individual families borrowed money for home construction and business development. Because of home construction and access to the global market, small businesses exploded, outpacing the production of large corporations. It became customary for people wanting to start a small business to borrow money from banks using the increase in equity in their home as collateral.

Total manufacturing capacity rapidly reached the highest level since the beginning of the Industrial Revolution. In turn, employees in these expanding industries created more jobs as they bought homes, spent their earnings, and created a demand for more consumer products.

Home construction in America continued to support the manufacturing sector even after other countries with emerging economies became competitors in global markets. It stimulated the industries that supplied materials, appliances, and home furnishings. It would have taken years for low-wage workers in manufacturing to dramatically increase domestic consumer demand and become a significant portion of the product consumer class without borrowing against future earnings.

The rapid growth in home construction accelerated the process of increasing prosperity. When millions of homebuyers borrow future earnings and spend the loan amount in a single year, the economy receives a boost that is not possible through a slow increase in manufacturing jobs.

For more than 200 years, economists and scholars have been debating how the use of capital and labor creates wealthy nations. Yet no one ever considered the impact on economic systems of people being encouraged to borrow money and invest in appreciating assets. This phenomenon was ignored even after it became common practice.

People around the world should study empirical data on how the construction of homes impacts the economy to better understand what could be accomplished in their country. Inflation often increases the net worth of a family because the home value increases with inflation.

However, do not assume that the increase in value merely represents the amount of inflation and that the value of the home, if adjusted for inflation, would produce funds that could not buy any more than at the time of purchase.

When a family sells a home and receives a return of equity that is 10 times the amount of their original down payment, it is very difficult to convince them they are actually no better off because the new price merely reflects the inflation or the reduction in the buying power of money. The value of existing homes often increases faster than the rate of inflation because of their appeal to new buyers.

For example, in 1949 a 1,000 square foot home just outside of New York City sold for approximately $11 per square foot, or $11,000.

If the value of that home increased at the average rate of the Consumer Price Index from 1949 to 2006, or 4.05%, today the home would cost $106,000. It would be difficult to find a 1,000 square foot home selling for less than $210 per square foot ($210,000) in the same area today. This means the cost of housing in the U.S. has increased an average of 5.64% per year since the mid 21st century. Put another way, housing prices have gone up 40% faster than inflation. If our average house had only one owner from 1949 to 2006, the buyer who put down 10% ($1,100) or less has realized an average increase in value of $4,200 per year. It is more likely that our 1949 house has had at least eight owners, but they all shared in the home's increase in value, with the amount varying, depending on when they purchased the home and how long they owned it.

The evidence was brought to light by more than fifty years of economic growth in the United States.

It changed our thinking about how to create economically viable societies and eradicate poverty in developing countries. Insured mortgage financing can literally raise the standard of living for an entire country. It has without question proved to be the key to creating prosperity by freeing people to participate in the economy, which is the true source of wealth for nations.

The growth of the American economy from 1945 to the mid-1970s was extraordinary. It is believed that the growth of small businesses (whose net value increased to $500 billion) is how poor families created a prosperous America.

When we consider the size of the U.S. economy in the late 1940s, we can see that growth in small businesses was a product of employment growth fueled primarily by loans for new home construction.

Contributions to the GDP by small businesses were more than six times the amount of the gains of the biggest corporations in America during the same period.

It was not these small businesses, often started in extremely poor households that energized the economy as some economists would have us believe. Any business, large or small, must have buyers with money before it can sell a product. From the mid 40s to the mid 70s, millions of homes were built. Billions of dollars poured into the economy, creating a need for products, many supplied by small businesses. To believe that financing an unincorporated small business, or any business, can greatly expand an economy simply by manufacturing new products or providing a new service is absurd. That has been tried in some struggling economies and it has failed. The demands for the consumer goods have to be established first.

If the mere addition of businesses through industrialization or other means were sufficient to create great prosperity, the industrialization of America would have made it happen prior to the 1950s. The process of industrialization had been gaining speed for more than 100 years when the Great Depression struck in 1929. However, the economy was so fragile that only a few industrial giants and the wealthy had sufficient resources to withstand the impact without major suffering. As Baumohl observed, a strong and well planned home building industry insures a nation's economy against such major disruptions.

OWNERSHIP IS NOT UNIQUE TO THE UNITED STATES

The most important lesson to draw from the empirical evidence of home building in the United States as the driving force behind unprecedented widespread prosperity is that this phenomenon is not unique to the United States. It has been repeated in a number of countries; countries as similar to the U.S. as Canada, and as different from the U.S. as Japan, Taiwan, South Korea, the United Kingdom, and Germany. It is now occurring in countries such as China. The common thread in these and other national success stories is the establishment of personal property rights guaranteed and enforced by the rule of law. The empirical evidence of home construction worldwide also supports this plan and demonstrates the power and effectiveness of the principles of participatory economics that have greatly increased the economic prosperity in developed countries.

TRADE CREATES JOBS NOT PROSPEROUS NATIONS

For many years there was a common belief that increasing imports from emerging economies would increase their manufacturing capacity and create jobs to a level that would begin to raise the level of prosperity. There is no question that trade increases jobs. Even though most of the jobs were at the lowest possible wage, the people were undoubtedly better off just because they had a job.

However, this was probably never one of the reasons behind granting aid and making loans to governments and corporations.

Undoubtedly it was to establish a means to increase the manufacturing capacity in emerging economies in a manner that reduced the manufacturing cost and increased profits for the foreign company.

Because of this approach, past and current efforts to help struggling countries through the use of foreign aid and loans have not resulted in an increase in prosperity. The people who live in these nations are thought of as abstractions, such as "labor" or "the work force," if they are thought of at all. Almost universally, prosperous countries extend foreign aid to governments and corporations in emerging nations in the hope that they will be able to energize their economies. This is an exclusionary process that attempts to build the economies of struggling countries. It assumes that people are not only subordinate but also dependent on the success of governments and corporations.

The underlying assumption is if an emerging country's national, regional and local governments and corporations become stronger and more dynamic through loans and foreign aid, the standard of living for those nation's citizens will rise.

This is the trade myth surrounding globalization. It is indeed a myth. Financing people in their efforts to invest in the economy does actually work.

The trade myth doesn't work because it fails to recognize the fundamental economic principle necessary for a nation to become prosperous; the people must become prosperous first. A major change in this thinking process is necessary if programs to eradicate poverty are to be successful.

In prosperous countries, governments and corporations derive their success as a product of the economic growth created by the people, when the people have the right to own private property and are free to borrow and invest.

Their ability to increase their income and aggregate demand is what sustains and supports governments and manufacturing corporations. Striving to achieve free trade globally at this time, when global unemployment is increasing, is not the answer. The theory that eliminating barriers to international sales of goods will raise the standard of living for all nations has not proven to be true, because the disparity between economies makes it impossible to reach agreement. The notion that "globalizing" trade automatically improves the economic viability of any country selling in the international marketplace lacks foundation, both as a principle and by empirical evidence.

It is true that countries entering a previously closed international market are able to create low-paying jobs that did not exist when it was shut out from the global marketplace.

However, the jobs do not provide the economic environment for the vast majority of the poorly paid population to become prosperous. Restricting wages to a level that binds the people to sub-human living conditions is cruel. In truth, all nations tilt the economic playing field in their favor to pay very low wages in underdeveloped countries. The August, 2006, collapse of the World Trade Organization's Doha Round of trade negotiations and subsequent disputes between developed and developing nations, is an example of why many people in the developing world view the term "globalization" with contempt. It demonstrates that countries are not willing to change trade polices while the disparity between national economies is so extreme.

Pulitzer Prize-winning economist Joseph Stiglitz, commented in his book *Fair Trade for All*[xii]

"…the international trade regime in many ways is disadvantageous to the developing countries."

This is a world Stiglitz observes has been moving very gradually towards reducing tariffs and restrictions on trade since the end of World War II. What creates this contradictory state of world trade affairs? Stiglitz writes,

"Some of the developed countries that have been the most ardent advocates of trade liberalization have been somewhat duplicitous in their advocacy.

> They have negotiated the reduction of tariffs and the elimination of subsidies for the goods in which they have a comparative advantage, but are more reluctant to open up their own markets and to eliminate their own subsidies in other areas where the emerging economies have an advantage."

The incredible maze of subsidies and tariffs established to protect various countries cannot be resolved using the current approach to economic development. It is necessary to adopt a new development plan which reduces the disparity between countries and within countries before continuing attempts to resolve trade issues.

Unfortunately, we have witnessed the effects of an incomplete understanding of how to apply free-market principles as international manufacturing corporations swept into many agriculturally based economies.

Too often governments and corporations in those underdeveloped countries have been given loans which failed to energize their economies. The empirical data shows that this inept approach to economic development has ushered in a form of globalization that promised, but has not delivered widespread prosperity.

Major loans to governments of emerging countries, in exchange for trade concessions, have sometimes created the illusion of greater prosperity. But far more often this creates chaos when the economy fails to expand, tax revenues do not increase, and the government is not able to repay the loan.

In the same way, imposing amateurish and naive banking regulations on emerging economies in attempts to stimulate economic activity has most often led to more financial disorder as evidenced by the many regional monetary crises that have erupted in recent years.

How then can economically weak nations ever hope to become stronger if international trade is not the solution? The answer is a different approach to creating prosperity by energizing domestic economies that are less dependent on foreign trade. Nations become prosperous when their people become prosperous through owning private property and private businesses. No nation can become economically independent and remain economically strong and prosperous if it does not make the health of its domestic economy the primary focus.

There are an enormous number of issues and problems that surround global economic development tend to reinforce. There is an erroneous idea that there is no practical solution that will accelerate the eradication of severe poverty.

Discussions and written analyses of global poverty consistently deal with statistics of starvation, disease, homelessness, lack of education, and the limited resources available to solve problems. How do we accelerate the positive political and economic changes that are already taking place? This proposed plan provides the means to meet the demands of the basic problems.

Until global poverty is substantially eradicated and product consumer demands increase, the difficulties surrounding the global economic disparities and world trade agreements will continue. As each country concentrates on improving their own struggling economy and protecting their domestic industry, the difficulties will only intensify.

When legal title is established either by grant or purchase, new land owners will have equity in the land that will serve as collateral for home construction loans.

The use of the equity in the property will reduce the disparity between nations as the level of income begins to increase. This is the process that will encourage new trade agreement, and further increase demands for consumer products.

.

PART IX

MORTGAGE INSURANCE AGENCIES

Mortgage insurance for home ownership is the key to establishing national prosperity in any nation that establishes protected private property rights. The insurance encourages mortgage lenders willing to finance lower income borrowers to make loans. This dramatically increases the number of lower income workers that qualify for a loan due to the protection it offers the lenders.

INSURED MORTGAGES

The history of home construction in the United States provides empirical evidence that the unprecedented increase in the standard of living across the entire country is primarily the result of insured mortgage financing which started the process sixty years ago. Insuring home mortgages was responsible for creating millions of jobs. The newly employed bought homes and began to save which raised the standard of living and greatly increased prosperity. Mortgage insurance made home ownership a reality for people from the lower income levels by ensuring them the right and opportunity to invest in private homes and personal businesses. Mortgage insurance created a practical system for the financial community to step forward and provide a means for the people to have access to capital so they could participate in the economy by investing in homes.

FINANCIAL INCENTIVES

Providing economic incentives for banks, governments, investors, and borrowers to invest in private property is an important aspect of eradicating severe global poverty.

Through the universal adoption of the proposed plan and the creation of International Mortgage Insurance Agencies, it is believed that trillions of dollars will become available to banks in struggling economies for the purpose of making loans for home construction.

The incentive, money loaned to banks in participating countries for home mortgages, in- creases the GDP. The opportunity to become more prosperous encourages governments in emerging countries to establish laws that permit and encourage the creation of a home building industry.

Lending billions of dollars to banks in emerging economies for home mortgages provides the governments with a reason to adopt laws that provide for and encourage private property ownership. At the same time the laws will protect borrowers and financing entities through strict adherence to the letter of the law.

Each individual family's freedom to invest, when encouraged and protected by law, provides them with an active role in the economic development of their nation. Freedom to invest in private property is the crucial freedom that raises the standard of living of all working families.

A common example is the acquisition of a home. The down payment of a home buyer can be 10% of the purchase price or less when insured financing is available. This permits the homebuyer to purchase an asset that not only is worth 10 to 20 times the amount of the down payment, but one that also increases in value over time. This appreciation in value protects the growing equity in the home during inflationary periods, while the total home value increases by multiples of the initial equity invested.

The rights to borrow and invest must be backed up by the government's protection of private property rights and supported by institutions that offer the opportunity and the resources to exercise those rights. People must have some place to live and a portion of their income, no matter how small, must go to meet that need. By investing in a home rather than renting, working families redirect that expenditure and begin the process of becoming prosperous by creating a growing personal net worth through the ownership of an appreciating asset.

When renters become homebuyers, the rent money turns into an investment: mortgage payments. This allows for saving money that is protected from inflation.

Low-cost mortgages with terms that permit the maximum number of working families to qualify for financing are essential to the success of participatory economics. Maximizing the number of borrowers by minimizing the cost of loans helps to energize the economy and accelerates the creation of a subsequent chain of new jobs for the unemployed. Insured home mortgages reduce the interest rate by reducing the risk to lenders.

Empirical evidence demonstrates the workability of implementing participatory economics as the core principle for spreading prosperity to all sectors of the economy, including government. The key to implementing participatory economics for the eradication of global poverty is the formation of additional International Mortgage Insurance Agencies to insure loans in emerging economies are patterned after existing and proven mortgage insurance formats. These agencies encourage the international financial community to make loans to banks in emerging economies. The funding of domestic banks empowers people by providing access to capital for all at a lower cost.

In 1947, the United States Congress enacted the Marshall Plan to help Europeans rebuild their cities which were shattered by World War II. The Marshall Plan increased the manufacturing capacity in the United States as it responded to the demands of Europe and the United States became the world's leading exporter.

However, although the increase in manufacturing created jobs for millions of Americans, the net worth of those workers and their families increased because they became homeowners, not because they found modest-wage employment.

Unlike current ineffective economic development strategies that finance governments and corporations so they can provide minimum wage jobs, participatory economics is a plan that finances people who are the homebuyers at all income levels. This will actually increase the net worth of the people in impoverished countries.

GUARANTEED TITLE OF OWNERSHIP RIGHTS

A country should have a well established process for proving ownership, based on a title report system. This is the number one priority for any government seeking money to eradicate poverty by attracting foreign investors. Before any homes can be constructed, a country must establish non-discriminating private property laws, real estate institutions, and legal procedures that fully guarantee the protection of private property rights through the rule of law. Implementing the principles of participatory economics internationally requires that the International Mortgage Insurance Agencies evaluate the degree of protection provided by the governments of countries applying for insurance.

INTERNATIONAL MORTGAGE INSURANCE

To protect against a loss when making mortgage loans, lenders purchase insurance from insurance companies who specialize in insuring lenders. It reduces the lender's risk for which the lender is willing to pay a fee to the insurance company.

Home construction in underdeveloped countries is possible when insured mortgage financing becomes available to working people in underdeveloped countries. Currently, mortgage insurers in the United States such as AIG, United Guaranty, and Glenworth Financial are already insuring loans in Mexico. Insuring loans for housing makes it possible to fund loans to people who would have not qualified otherwise. Expenditure of the funds for home building creates the demand for more consumer products. It is the same economic development process that evolved in the United States in the late 1940s and 50s and continues to this day.

The innovation of mortgage insurance unleashed a viable construction industry and is the undeniable driving force in a healthy U.S. economy. The process of insuring the repayment of home mortgage funds for hundreds of millions of people over the past fifty years increased the number that qualified for a loan. Because of mortgage insurance, the interest rates were lowered and the amortization period was extended to reduce the amount of the monthly payments, making home ownership possible for the lower income groups. Employment in the housing industry created new product consumers, and a demand for all types of products, which in turn created more jobs, resulting in the growth of the manufacturing industry and national prosperity.

The first and most important step is to expand international mortgage insurance to all lenders willing to invest in countries with protected private property laws that wish to participate. This will encourage investors to make loans to domestic banks in emerging economies specifically for building homes.

International mortgage insurance will make it possible to fund an enormous global home building enterprise in underdeveloped countries as hundreds of millions of jobs are established. Imagine eradicating severe global poverty by providing a home for every family now living without any protection or in temporary shacks with other families.

REINSURING MORTGAGES

The process for funding insured home mortgages in underdeveloped countries will be the same used in America and other countries. If it proves necessary, the Overseas Private Investment Corporation, (OPIC), an agency of the United States government, plus other international agencies, could reinsure the top 10-15% of each mortgage loan, providing additional risk coverage to the international mortgage insurers and the financing community. International mortgage insurance companies would sell insurance to local banks and be partially reinsured by OPIC type agencies. Insured mortgages would then be funded by local banks through real estate escrow companies with title management abilities, similar to those established in most countries that have private property rights, providing yet another job sector for the unemployed.

Insured mortgages will prove to be crucial for adopting a global economic development plan which permits the newly employed to also become investors in their own asset.

The plan is not just a theory. It is the adoption of a viable, existing system that has created unbelievable wealth in the United States.

INTERNATIONAL AGREEMENTS

The following provides some preliminary thoughts for discussion on the fundamental terms and conditions of the binding international agreements that will be required. There will be a need for international agreements between governments, participating banks, real estate institutions, corporate sponsors, mortgage brokers, and stock exchanges for the attraction of the International Mortgage Insurance Agencies.

1. **GOVERNMENT GUARANTEES**. For this plan to be successful the International Mortgage Insurance Agencies should not require guarantees of repayment by governments in participating countries. Except to the extent the participating national government insures local deposits in local banks, and guarantees title to private property, the government's credit will not be a criterion. The loans should stand on the merits of the terms of the agreements.

It is crucial to relieve participating governments of guarantee requirements. In the past, economic development strategies have imposed severe restrictions and limitations on borrowing countries. Major financial crises arose when governments were unable to fund debt payments due to a lack of increase in the prosperity of their economy. Not including a government guarantee in the mortgage process avoids interference from foreign agencies while achieving the original intent of strategies

2. LOCAL INVESTORS. A significant portion of domestic bank funds should come from government as well as private sources within participating countries once opportunities for local, insured, and protected investments become available.

Domestic banks can purchase mortgage insurance for funds deposited locally to protect the local residents buying mortgage-backed bonds. Through the utilization of adjustable rate mortgages, local investors will be able to reduce their risk of local inflation. This economic development plan would also allow a portion of the mortgage funds to go to government services indirectly for the construction infrastructure and services which will help to strengthen the economy.

3. FOREIGN INVESTORS. In addition to local inflation, a risk which can be partially offset by adjustable interest rates on the mortgages, the foreign investor's risks are increased because of fluctuation in the exchange of the two currencies. This problem can be mitigated to some degree by utilizing traditional foreign exchange forwards, arguably the tool of choice for hedging. In some cases, synthetic hedges can be utilized, although these are less desirable unless managed properly.

4. TAX REVENUE. Government revenues increase enormously from taxes on the disbursement of construction loans and on the subsequent rollover of funds moving through the economy to buy consumer products manufactured domestically.

5. LOCAL DEVELOPERS. Some of the more affluent will undoubtedly acquire large tracts of land and sponsor new construction companies and other new businesses following the passage of necessary land-use laws and the establishment of institutions to support the development and sale of homes. A nation's economy is energized by the employment created when financially established domestic investors are encouraged to invest in their own countries, instead of investing in the stock market of a foreign country.

6. MORTGAGE COLLATERAL FUND. As an integral part of encouraging IMIAs to open office in emerging economies, it may be necessary to establish a Mortgage Collateral fund for each participating country, capitalized by governments, development agencies, foundations, and individuals seeking a means to use aid and international lending more effectively.

This would be a reserve of funds needed to provide reinsurance or back up insurance for the top 10% to 20% of the loan made by the International Mortgage Insurance Agencies. The Collateral Fund could be a non-profit organization that pledges the Mortgage Collateral Fund as security for mortgage insurance issued to banks in participating countries for home financing. The collateralized guarantee encourages mortgage insurance agencies and international lenders to lend to banks for the sole purpose of making home loans to homebuyers.

Contributing foreign aid to the Mortgage Collateral Fund leverages the impact foreign aid has on economic development. Such contributions enable the international banking community to lend struggling economies twenty times the amount of foreign aid contributed to the Collateral Fund.

It is expected that a major portion of the capital for each country's Mortgage Collateral Fund would come from contributions by national governments and international agencies wanting to sponsor specific projects.

They would have the right to direct their foreign aid and/or economic development funds to a Mortgage Collateral Fund specific to a sponsored project. Foreign governments, international agencies, and corporate sponsors would have the capability of leveraging their funds by contributing to the Mortgage Collateral Fund as an alternative to directly lending to governments and making direct investments. Money contributed may be earmarked for a specific fund/project in a participating country or offered without specific instructions. The Agency would allocate unspecified contributions to each country's Mortgage Collateral Fund based on need.

The money would be held in the Mortgage Collateral Fund for each country indefinitely. Contributions to each of the specific Mortgage Collateral Funds would increase as home construction raises the standard of living and the demand for mortgage loans increases. A growing economy encourages other non-profits and governments to consider leveraging of their available funds, assist emerging economies by contributing to the Mortgage Collateral Fund. It is a self-perpetuating process and as more jobs are created, the number of qualified buyers will grow. Demonstrated prosperity in the initial participating countries will increase confidence in the Mortgage Collateral Fund concept.

7. BANK CREDIT WORTHINESS. Initially, banks in participating countries will solicit capital directly from the international financial community, offering collateral for loans in the form of insured mortgages made directly to homebuyers.

Participating banks will have to prove creditworthiness with sufficient management capability to issue and process mortgages. The creditworthiness of a participating bank is evaluated based on the creditworthiness of each corporate sponsor and subsequent borrower. It is anticipated that the International Mortgage Insurance Agencies will act together as manager of the collateral held in trust for each sponsor and project, and be responsible for evaluating credit of participating banks. Participating banks will maintain credit ratings on borrowers and sponsors for each specific project. As the international banking community acquires more banking interests in foreign countries, professional banking practices should reduce any problems with creditworthiness of participating banks.

8. **SALE OF BONDS.** A significant source of bank funds could also come from private investors within participating countries through the purchase of mortgage-backed bonds. Participating banks are permitted to sell mortgages to local and international mortgage brokers to recapitalize their lending process. Investors purchasing mortgage-backed bonds internationally are entitled to all guarantees and protections offered for mortgage-backed bond sold locally. The legal structure of mortgages must meet international lending standards set by the International Mortgage Insurance Agencies to insure the feasibility of mortgage-backed bond sales internationally.

9. **TAX-FREE BONDS.** Investment bankers will only be approved to sell the mortgage-backed bonds in countries where the governments permit the yield on the bonds to be tax-free income.

This process improves the marketability of mortgage-backed bonds while lowering the interest rates charged to borrowers in developing countries. Tax-free bonds encourage people everywhere to become investors and to take part in the eradication of poverty by financing the economic development of participating countries. Tax-free bonds also ensure the lowest possible interest rate for borrowers within the economic limitations of each specific country. Taxing income from bonds in countries where mortgage-backed bonds are offered would impose an unnecessary increase in interest rate on struggling borrowers in developing countries. The yield on bonds may vary for each participating country, depending on a particular country's economic stability and the country's degree of protection for private property rights.

10. **MORTGAGE INSURANCE FEES.** The initial cost of insurance and the mortgage interest rate will vary according to the anticipated risk of making loans in each country. The fees charged for

mortgage insurance will be adjusted as homeowners in each country demonstrate the ability to reduce the foreclosure rate to a minimum standard. This serves as an incentive for governments to enforce the law and to encourage prudent financial policies in an attempt to lower the interest rate on mortgages, thereby increasing the number of prospective homebuyers that would qualify.

11. MORTGAGE POOLS. As is current practice, participating banks will replace foreclosed mortgages with new mortgages as a means of maintaining the full value of the pool of mortgage backed bonds sold on stock exchanges internationally.

12. HOMEOWNERS INSURANCE. The International Mortgage Insurance Agencies would set construction standards to certify that homes are built to appropriate quality specifications for each level of income. This is to ensure that the worth of the home is commensurate with the amount of the insured loan. Since the total loans to any domestic bank will be the sum of the amount of loans made for specific homes, the possibility of corruption is vastly reduced. Local authorities approve the architectural design and project planning. All borrowers are required to maintain homeowners insurance to protect themselves and lenders from loss or damage to the home.

13. SPONSORS CONTRIBUTIONS. Governments and/or corporations sponsoring specific development projects are required to deposit five percent of their requested amount of financing in the Mortgage Collateral Fund established for each project sponsored. Combining a portion of the general Mortgage Collateral Fund held by the Agency with funds directed by a sponsor assists in meeting the collateral requirement for each specific project's insurance.

Each country is evaluated based on its borrower's repayment rate, the national foreclosure rate, and the balance of the collateral allocated to that country.

After five years, or upon completion of a project, if the rate of foreclosure does not exceed the Universal International Standard established by the International Mortgage Insurance Agencies, the money deposited by the sponsors of the project is returned to the contributor. This incentive gives sponsors a stake in the long-term creditworthiness of borrowers.

14. INCREASING THE NUMBER WHO QUALIFIES. Mortgage insurance reduces the risk of lending and consequently lowers the interest rate on loans. In addition, the sale of tax-free bonds backed by insured mortgages lowers the yield requirements of investors who buy the bonds. These two organizational constraints combine to lower the interest rate charged to borrowers. The lower the interest rate, the lower the amortizing mortgage payment, and therefore the higher the number of borrowers who qualify.

15. RESALE OF FORECLOSURES. The International Mortgage Insurance Agencies will pay claims on foreclosures with money from the Mortgage Collateral Fund if necessary. Typically, however, insurance claims are minimized if not eliminated by participating banks reselling of foreclosed homes without loss. Replacing the mortgages on homes repossessed by the bank with new mortgages maintains the integrity of the bond pool.

Experience with people whose home is their only asset provides ample evidence that the probability of foreclosure will be very low, particularly as economies improve.

Owning a home is such an incredible opportunity for people that new owners will do everything possible to avoid foreclosure, including taking in family members and others as tenants. The rate of foreclosure is not a problem unless a major incident such as a war or terrorism disrupts the economy.

16. CONDITIONS FOR QUALIFYING. A great many prospective homebuyers in emerging economies have not established credit and/or have not worked for others as regular employees.

Many operate private businesses without licenses. Both groups are not on the tax rolls, working in what is often called the unmonitored economy. To reach the largest number of people possible, it is necessary that people who are unable to prove their income level have a means to qualify for a loan.

Many are currently renting which establishes the first level of payment if they are not living in a shack on land as poachers. Secondly, the buyers will be required to report at least a portion of their income and establish a savings account. They will make monthly deposits in the bank, which equal or exceed the monthly payment on the home they intend to buy. This will continue until their savings account balance is high enough to make the down payment on the home. The account will serve two purposes. It will demonstrate the homebuyer's ability to make the anticipated monthly payments and will provide the funds necessary for the down payment.

17. **PROJECT SPONSORS**. Sponsors of projects will be able to contribute funds to the Mortgage Collateral Fund established to support the insurance commitment to the international banking community. The sponsor's contribution leverages the impact they have on the economy of participating countries by increasing the amount of funds that can be loaned to local banks.

Contributing to the Fund preserves the capital of sponsors by eliminating the need for sponsors or governments to loan money directly to the banks for making mortgage loans. When available capital is deposited in the Mortgage Collateral Fund, the principal is not depleted, as is the case when sponsors act alone and make loans directly.

This multiplies the impact of the sponsor's capital because the international banking community loans a multiple of the Mortgage Collateral Fund to the sponsor's project. The investment of the contributions held in the Mortgage Collateral Fund creates a growing fund, based on the investment income and subject to the viability of the sponsor's profit.

18. LONG TERM COMMITMENT. It is critical that domestic and international manufacturing companies have sufficient lead-time to establish manufacturing capacity and delivery systems as they make plans to respond to what could be a very rapid increase in demand for materials, equipment, parts, appliances, and furnishings. This reduces the risk of uncontrolled inflation due to the anticipated dramatic increase in aggregate demand.

Manufacturers must also have confidence that there will be an ongoing increase in the number of homes built each year. There must be a long-term commitment to the housing program. This will sustain an increasing demand if local and international manufacturers and distributors in participating countries are to be encouraged to build up their manufacturing capacity. Once demand is established and begins to increase annually at a predictable rate, more manufacturers and distributors will come into each market. This will also help to reduce inflationary trends. Once the potential increase in sales volume is established, financing of manufacturing expansion should not be a problem.

19. AVAILABLE CAPITAL. At the time of this writing, the international financial community has the funds to make sizeable investments in domestic banks in participating economies.

In our history, there never has been such a tremendous amount of capital languishing, while investors seek viable investments. Mortgage insurance lessens the risk for the international banking community as it takes on the responsibility of financing the eradication of poverty. The banking community will oversee the process, using prudent and proven lending practices that can be controlled and standardized internationally.

Governments and international agencies have money to lend and to donate as direct aid. They must look favorably on the opportunity to leverage the impact these funds can have on poverty by contributing to a Mortgage Collateral Fund. For example, an initial $10 billion in foreign aid and development funds redirected to the Mortgage

Collateral Fund could result in one hundred billion dollars in loans to homeowners globally depending on the ratio to be established. Initially, the ratio of total mortgage funds to the Mortgage Collateral Fund could be as low as ten to one. However, as loans mature, the ratio can be increased as the established standard for the foreclosure rate is achieved.

ESTABLISHING A PROCESS

The following is a list of steps to be considered in the establishment of International Mortgage Insurance Agencies.

Establish an agreement of International Mortgage Insurance Agencies to participate in the program and the Mortgage Collateral Fund, independent of governmental and banking interests.

1. Sign up governments and international agencies committed to eradicating global poverty who will agree to contribute funds to the Mortgage Collateral Fund for projects they wish to sponsor.
2. With insurance agreements in place, reach agreement with the international banking community to agree to loan funds to banks in participating countries they approve, subject to the guarantee of the International Mortgage Insurance Agencies.
3. Countries applying for participation must establish laws that clarify, or if necessary, establish private property rights to protect the international banking community. Laws must also be structured to increase the feasibility of borrowing and investing in homes and small businesses by providing tax incentives for homeowners that reduce the total out-of-pocket-cost of borrowing.

4. Banks in participating countries must qualify with the International Mortgage Insurance Agencies as insured mortgage lenders for home construction before approaching the international banking community for funds. This requirement could be waived if insurance is not required. This could become a possibility should domestic mortgage insurance materialize or if insurance is no longer required, based on the prosperity of people in the participating country.

5. International and domestic investors, investing in participating countries must then step forward and take responsibility as sponsors of projects to form and construct housing developments. They must apply to participating banks for funds and deposit their required contribution with the Mortgage Collateral Fund.

6. National governments that wish to support the program by allowing the sale of bonds backed by insured mortgages must pass laws to eliminate the tax on income from the sale of the bonds.

7. The qualified mortgage brokers must establish procedures for the purchase and sale of tax-free insured mortgage-backed bonds on international stock exchanges.

8. Men and women in all countries who desire to assist in eradicating global poverty must step forward and purchase tax-free bonds backed by insured mortgages on new homes in developing countries.

PART X

ECONOMIC TRENDS

Prosperity for all people of any nation becomes a reality when the people of that nation resolve to act and to insist that the government of that nation provide protected private property rights and create an entirely new economic environment that enables The Twelve Economic Principles That Create Prosperous Nations to become part of the economy.

David R. Johns

ECONOMIC TRENDS

The evolution of an economic society based on participatory economics changes many of the cultural customs and business procedures. The changes produce new economic trends and a new vocabulary for doing business. They serve to establish a totally new attitude about working, saving, and investing. The following are some of the current trends that indicate the nature of an economy based on a home building industry.

Adopting a new plan for stabilizing the global economy provides an opportunity to increase prosperity for all and reduce economic disparity within countries and between countries. At the beginning of 2006, we watched the global economy continued to slow as demand for goods by Western consumers began to taper off. Most indicators failed to illustrate the extent to which the international economy had become overburdened with consumer products. Total global sales were beginning to flatten and in many areas, total sales of consumer products were falling rapidly. Global inventories of manufacturers began to climb. Manufacturing economies that provided the majority of consumer products in the past were beginning to feel competition from emerging nations joining the World Trade Organization. The economic indicators provide no evidence that the former level of global manufacturing can be restored without new consumers and the demands they will place on the global economy. It appears that there will be an increase in unemployment because of the lack of a solution if this proposed plan is not adopted.

EXCESSIVE PERSONAL DEBT
LOWERS DEMAND

Increasing short term personal debt is not an alternative for producing consumer demand. An examination into the relationship between personal debt and the level of employment worldwide provides insight into the conditions that may arise in emerging economies as the economies begin to improve. In the past ten years, the average personal debt of Americans has increased over 50% to an all-time high of over $7,000 per capita. At one point, it totaled more than two trillion dollars. The increase in personal debt was a major reason that consumer demand increased and imports per capita hit an all time high. However, this was a short cycle that disrupted the economy when the credit lines hit the limit and the number of jobs had not increased.

In the United States over the last ten years, personal savings shrunk as consumers rushed out to buy the latest versions of the newest products. Many Americans took out equity loans on their homes and spent personal savings. This decreased their net worth, the equity in their home, while the consumer products they bought began losing value immediately after purchase. As the people become employed in the emerging economies, the total personal debt will increase imports. However, excess personal debt can also be part of another slow down in the global economy in the future.

Considering the amount of total debt held by Americans, it is unlikely there will be a new surge of consumer buying in the U.S. in the near future which will restrict imports.

The United States cannot continue to provide the major support for emerging economies because United States buying power for consumer products is reaching its limit. Strong evidence of this is the extreme and damaging pressures placed on lenders to lower interest rates and qualifications on home loans. This has resulted in an oversupply of homes that will prevent any major home building in the near future.

GDP – THE UNITED STATES

Other countries are already feeling the effects of the slowdown in the United States economy. **The World Fact Book** data released by the **Central Intelligence Agency** provides statistics on how the economies of different countries are changing each year. The United States imported more than $1.56 trillion worth of products or about $5,200 per capita based on a population of 310,000,000 citizens in 2009. This is an amount equal to 10.93% of the $14.26 trillion GDP that year. The United States Gross Domestic product was estimated at $48,499 per capita in 2009 while GDP real growth rate was only 2.4% for the year. The GDP for 2011is projected to be around 2.0 %.

The United States exported approximately $1.046 trillion in consumer products in 2009, or $3,400 per capita based on a population of 310,000,000. In other words, the United States spent almost $1,800 per capita or $5.58 billion in 2009, buying more imports than exports sold, which supported manufacturing in other nations. This cannot continue when the current personal debt is believed to exceed the capability of the Americans to repay in the event of a worsening eco- nomic down turn.

By comparison, China imported only $954.3 billion in foreign-made products while exporting $1.204 trillion. That figure represents 13.7% of China's $8.758 trillion GDP in exports, adjusted for Purchasing Power Parity. China's GDP was estimated at only $6,600 per capita while the GDP real growth rate was 8.7%. Although China's GDP/capita is much lower than the U.S., the rate of increase in GDP per year is much higher than the United States. Their GDP/capita could equal the U.S. in twelve to fifteen years if there is not a major change in the structure of the United States economy. This is a major shift in the global economic power structure. At the same level of GDP/capita, the total Gross Domestic Product in China would be over five times that of the United States because their population is five times larger.

INCREASING LABOR COST

All emerging economies become victims of their own success if they fail to establish a domestic economy with the profits from international sales. As soon as an emerging nation sells more manufactured goods internationally, its factory workers wages increase. Unfortunately, in a relatively short period, the rising wages causes the products to be less competitive in the global market and countries begin to lose manufacturing jobs. America lost jobs as wages began to increase and exports declined. Fortunately, America had established a strong economy driven by home construction.

The same thing happened to other economies after they took over manufacturing for export from America.

Jobs continue to move from country to country as each new emerging economy expands and the improved standard of living forces an increase in manufacturing wages. New countries joining the World Trade Organization continue the process.

In America, as world competition began to take over manufacturing contracts, it became necessary to locate new manufacturing plants in smaller developing communities. Lower cost housing in the South and West attracted lower wage earners, beginning as early as the 1950s when Motorola opened plants in Phoenix, Arizona. A number of high-tech manufacturers have followed in an attempt to hold wages down. World competition continues to drive the high-tech industry to lower cost labor markets. Planning for the relocation of manufacturing to less expensive domestic labor markets within countries where possible has become part of the new planning paradigm for emerging economies as countries with lower cost labor enter the global free market.

As the economy begins to recover due to the global home building industry, it is expected the labor cost worldwide will begin to climb. This will be good for both the developing counties and the more industrial economies. It is important that the disparity in wages globally be reduced as part of employing people in home construction and in manufacturing to meet the demand for imports of material and equipment for homes. Reducing economic disparities improves relationships between countries and increases world trade.

CHINA'S JOB LOSS

China is an example of what happens as an emerging economy begins increasing its manufacturing capability and raising its GDP per capita. As manufacturing spread from Japan and South Korea to China, prices on exportation of products continued to drop. The resulting global buying frenzy supported astonishing growth in Asia s manufacturing capacity, which brought a measure of prosperity to millions of people in Asian countries. China was able to raise the standard of living for 25% of its population by selling consumer products internationally. It now appears that China will not be able to continue to use this same process to raise the standard of living for the other 75% of its people with the decline in demand for consumer products as well as limited numbers of product consumers globally. In an attempt to maintain a remarkable annual GDP, China is implementing a massive home building industry, which has created millions of new jobs in recent years.

According to some sources, China began losing manufacturing jobs due to a decline in exports in 2004 when employment in this sector dropped by 15 million. The ongoing job loss in export manufacturing in China is due to lower global demand for consumer products and the competition from newly emerging countries joining the WTO and entering the global trade market.

China is using profits from exports to expand the nation's infrastructure to support their efforts in home building and office buildings.

This process provided millions of construction jobs in addition to those in manufacturing, which prepared the basis for home construction and established an increasingly stable domestic economy which is less dependent on foreign trade.

Labor rates in China are beginning to increase in manufacturing and home construction. This is reflected in the higher prices for their exports. This may occur more slowly than might be expected since their export sales will be sluggish due to the financial crisis restricting consumer demand.

MANUFACTURING JOBS ARE NOT A SOLUTION

It is not possible to increase the number of buyers in the product consumer class of any given country simply by increasing the number of people employed in manufacturing products for domestic consumption. The ratio of buyers to workers must continually increase to keep pace with the increased production of consumer goods. These new buyers must have jobs outside of manufacturing. One hundred newly employed workers will manufacture more than the same one hundred employees can afford to buy. Each country seeking to increase the GDP must establish a method that substantially increases the number of product consumers domestically by some means other than creating jobs to manufacture goods for export. This is why the home building industry is the key to the stabilization of every economy.

SMALL HANDICRAFT LOANS ARE NOT A SOLUTION

Making very small loans to small businesses or directly to craftsmen in underdeveloped countries in an attempt to raise the standard of living is not a viable economic development plan.

There are not enough domestic buyers for the new products of the small businesses. Currently, in order for small businesses in underdeveloped countries to succeed, they must increase the volume and be able to sell to consumers on the international market.

DOMESTIC BUYERS OF CONSUMER PRODUCTS

A better way to develop small businesses in underdeveloped countries is to create a growing class of domestic buyers by loaning money for home construction. This infuses the economy with cash in the hands of the people, not government. Domestic banks financing homes infuse capital directly into the economy at the consumer level, utilizing long-term borrowing. This has been the foundation of small business growth in America and other developed nations.

Mechanization and modern agricultural practices have made it possible for a very small percentage of the work force to raise 100% of the food necessary to feed the entire population of a prosperous country.

In the United States, less than 2% of the work force of 139 million is employed in farming and related industries. Losing farm related jobs is a serious problem as developing nations become prosperous.

They have mechanized farms and adopted new growing methods. The number of people leaving the farms over the past thirty years has created unemployment in and around cities.

The further reduction in farm employment due to mechanization will be a major problem for emerging economies; however, mechanization is the only way the standard of living can be increased for farmers.

In China, hundreds of millions of people live and work in rural communities. Estimates indicate that as many as 10,000,000 people migrate to the cities annually looking for work because of the mechanization of farming. Widespread conversion to mechanized farming in emerging economies will cause unmanageable unemployment problems unless another domestic industry such as home building is established. The farmers in China are waiting until their home building economy and manufacturing expands further to the west just as manufacturing in the United States has done over the past fifty years.

In South America, millions of people have moved from rural areas to cities and have not been able to find work. On the outskirts of cities around the world, billions of people are hungry for the opportunity to work. Government owned industries have stifled the growth of the economy at a time when millions are starving.

To energize the global economy and provide jobs for the out-of-work farmers, it is necessary to increase the number of product consumers in each emerging country by expanding employment in a sector other than manufacturing for export. Adding three to four billion new consumers to the marketplace would double the number of manufacturing jobs worldwide.

If it were possible to add three billion people to the product consumer class, the changes in the economics of global development would completely alter the debate over globalization and trade negotiations.

International trade is an entirely different process when the people of emerging economies are not so critically dependent on manufacturing for export. Domestic manufacturing becomes a major employer when people have money to spend for construction materials and appliances due to construction lending. Energizing the economies in emerging economies tends to reduce the economic disparity between countries.

The banks in any country participating in the International Mortgage Insurance program have the opportunity to increase their borrowing capacity from the international banking community at lower rates because the funds loaned to homebuyers are insured. This increases the viability of participating banks by strengthening and stabilizing the lending process. Participating local banks will have the opportunity to utilize the mortgage insurance process for the loans funded domestically. Banks will no longer have to make deposits in foreign banks due to the lack of opportunities for domestic investment.

The eradication of poverty and the development of prosperous economies depend greatly on the banks in participating countries expanding and becoming the managers responsible for the home loan process. International banking will become an entirely different industry with the advent of International Mortgage Insurance. It offers the opportunity to invest in the eradication of poverty and increase global commerce by depositing capital in domestic bank for the purchase of insured home loans.

The international sale of tax-free mortgage-backed bonds to participating domestic banks will be a source to replenish capital for home construction and will add to the viability of the banks.

International agencies, foreign governments, and private foundations can leverage their impact on poverty by contributing to the Mortgage Collateral Fund. These contributions ensure the continued growth of the Fund and increase the amount of lending by the international banking community. Annual lending by the international banking community could exceed twenty times the total amount held in the Mortgage Collateral Fund. This viable process for financing families through participating banks far exceeds the amounts currently available for direct funding. Contributions to the Mortgage Collateral Fund are leveraged when the loan are ten to twenty times the amount of the contributions. Leveraging funds intended to help people in developing economies accelerates the eradication of poverty.

DOMESTIC INVESTORS

Researchers have established the fact that millions of hardworking people in emerging economies have become wealthy. Most of these upper income groups in emerging countries have no opportunity to invest their wealth within their own countries. Many elect to hold their money in foreign banks and invest in stocks and other investments in more economically free countries. This will change when countries participate in this economic development plan.

Once governments around the world decide to incorporate the legal changes necessary to permit international financing of a home building industry, these same investors will be a major force in launching the process that eradicates poverty.

With the establishment of laws that fully employ the principles of participatory economics, it becomes possible for people in higher income groups to sell their existing homes and build larger, more modern homes. This is the natural pattern of growth and expansion in an economically free nation, and it begins when people are free to invest in their own economies. Initially constructing homes for those with money and/or jobs starts the process and creates jobs for future homebuyers.

Opportunities will also open up to invest in land and develop services necessary for home building. There will be investment opportunities in manufacturing facilities to increase capacity in response to the demands of homebuyers. In the future, the best opportunities for investment globally will be in participating countries because of the rapid expansion of their economies. People will move to participating countries as the economy begins to expand because the emerging economies will need skilled workers, businessmen, and educators. Think of the subcontractor trades that must be improved; engineering firms and companies will be needed to establish ownership and to process the titles of homes, community planning, and real estate.

PART XI

CITIES FOR THE FUTURE

The primary goal of every new design concept for the expansion of a city or the creation of a new city must be the elimination of planning concepts that have contributed to the creation of unsustainable, dysfunctional societies and crime in the past.

NEW VILLAGES FOR HOMES

The implantation of the proposed worldwide home building plan will create new civilizations that will more than triple the number of people having homes in existing and new cities. Studies must be done to avoid repeating the problems that plague cities today. A few short comments on current problem provide an idea of the magnitude of research necessary to prevent repletion of past errors. The current highly developed population centers support approximately two billion people. There are at least another four billion that cannot afford to enjoy the luxury of living as part of a modern city.

As the prosperity increases these new workers will naturally require the same goods/services and real estate as the current consumers. However, there will be twice as many people, over four billion people in the short term and another three billion over the next forty to fifty years. Current modern cities support two billion and the population is expected to be approaching 10 billion in fifty years; that is an increase of eight billion people that will become prosperous or four times as many that are now consumers. This would mean that the total population will require five times as many city services, buildings, and facilities as currently exist.

Currently according to the magazine "Fastcompany" China alone needs 500 new cities each with a population of 1,000,000 or more people. The U.S. Company, Cisco, is joint venturing with Stan Gale to construct twenty new cities in India and China in the near future along the lines of New Songdo City being built in Korea.

This projected growth in the number of large cities gives rise to another major debate. How should these cities be planned, engineered, and constructed? We need significant improvement in how cities are to be developed to provide better housing. Building this many cities of this size will require enormous amounts of natural resources and energy unless a new concept for cites is adopted.

COST OF LIVING

There are a number of concerns. The cost of energy needed to service the buildings is enormous. The greatest importance to the people who will live and work in the expanded or new cites is the cost of living. In the future, if the impoverished become part of the product consumer class, all of the hundreds of emerging cities will be competing with each other for business. In a global economy, where the economic disparity between nations is dramatically reduced, the opportunity to provide goods and services becomes available to all businesses in every city. The economic disparity that exists between cities today will continue to be a problem. One of the determining factors that will establish a competitive edge will be the variance in the cost of labor. As evident for the past fifty years, the cities with the lower labor cost are the dominant force in the evolving trade economy. Planning a city that is expensive to live in will be a disservice to those forced to live there if they cannot manage to earn enough to pay the higher cost.

SOCIAL COHESION

There were large cities in the United States prior to the 1950s that had developed around a high-rise approach to design, some included skyscrapers.

However, the current major city landscapes that have evolved over the last fifty years are now surrounded by large urban areas known as suburban sprawl. The experiences with this evolutionary process and the total cityscapes that have emerged indicate that we have created enormous problems for the people living in them. Many planners, engineers, architects, and environmentalists believe it to be impractical if cities continue to expand as in the past or new cities are planned and constructed using the existing paradigm as a pattern for future development.

Unfortunately, the planning of the center of the cities and their suburban communities has created a situation in which it is possible for the people to live in an environment that permits complete anonymity. People can come and go to work and shopping and never interact with neighbors or others in the community where they live. In the cities, it is very possible to have a minimum of personal contact with fellow employees or shoppers. Living in complete anonymity within cities with limited social interaction is believed by many to be a major cause of our social problems today.

A NEW URBAN DESIGN

There are many proposed city plans for the future. Under this plan, the housing will be mostly condominiums. Some will be based on high density with twenty or more floors. Some homes could be located in new small, lower density communities.

In the United States, there are emerging urban designs that provide for small communities within major metropolitan areas. Each community has retail centers on a small town scale plus offices, commercial buildings, and numerous types and size of residential units. The concept has been developed to create numerous small and interacting communities within a very large metropolitan area. The success of these new designs has been extraordinary. They could contain medium density as well has high rise buildings depending on the availability of land and the needed increase in housing. Because many of the services and the offices are within walking distance of the homes, walking the streets is very desirable and offers opportunities to interact with others living in the "villages" in the same manner.

There must be a new design for cities which encourage the interaction of people to a more intense degree than in the past to reduce living cost and increase social interaction. The opportunity to have a "Social Network" on the internet for those that live within a small village creates an opportunity for more personal communication and face to face interaction. This approach provides an excellent opportunity to reduce the size of retail stores, schools, churches, and businesses to a scale that creates repeated interaction and cooperation which is essential for a healthy social environment.

NATURAL RESOURCES

Increasing the level of prosperity to the point that serve global poverty is eradicated will consume a very large amount of natural resources. Once four billion additional people begin work and play much like the more affluent do today the current annual consumption of natural resources will double.

As pointed out above the projections for the future indicate an increase in population of at least another four billion people in the next forty to fifty years. This will result in a second major increase in the consumption of natural resources. This assumes that once we have a new global economic development paradigm that eradicates poverty it will provides jobs for future generations in the same manner.

It must be obvious to everyone who understands the projected increase in demand for natural resources that we must get serious about the environmental and natural resource issues that we are facing. We will have to develop a new global plan for conservation and use of natural resources that will include new methods for meeting the demands for jobs and housing.

EPILOGUE
WE KNOW NOW

There has been no major global plan adopted in the past to correct the inhumane living conditions for the billions of people on this planet who have lived in poverty for their entire lives. No program has been implemented because it was universally believed that there was no economic development plan big enough in scope to deal with such a complex problem. We know now that building homes as defined herein is a development plan encompassing basic principles of development that will create hundreds of millions of jobs and eradicate systemic poverty.

If we fail to change our attitude toward solving the problems of global employment and poverty now, we will be faced with the consequences of a collision between two opposing economic development philosophies described in Chapter 1. Two different economic development theories are leading billions of people down divergent paths.

One group of countries, ruled by leaders seeking personal wealth and power through political dominance, are obsessed with the desire to manipulate the people in their countries and those in other countries according to their personal beliefs. They seek to control the lives of the people by using misleading information and pretending to be for the good of the people while using hate, violence and even terrorism in some countries to intimidate and impose their will.

In some countries, these leaders speak of change and imply their plan for leveling incomes and redistributing wealth through government taxation and spending is the path to prosperity.

In truth their plans are destroying jobs and investment opportunities for the people while putting money in their own pockets. They are just using the political argument as a means of enriching themselves.

Another group of leaders, recognizing opportunities for peace and prosperity for all nations are offering economic freedom to their people by permitting private property rights, providing financing, and encouraging business development and a home building industry.

It is impossible for these two worldviews to co-exist because one leads to wars and enslavement while the other leads to economic freedom, global prosperity, and peace for all. To avoid a global catastrophe, it is necessary to forget past grievances, both real and imaginary, and those created by propaganda and differences in political and religious beliefs.

Each nation must have the right to claim its own unequivocal sovereignty and be able to take independent action without dependence on a global government or international financing entities. It is sufficient that we all agree that the universe, this planet, and humanity were created by an infinite intelligence. There are natural humane laws which we all must obey if we are live in peace. Those include love and respect for each other, honesty in our relations, a commitment to peace, and prosperity for all. No one has greater worth than another. Each of us wants the same thing, to be able to protect and preserve our natural rights, our families, and our nation.

The conflict between economic theories can be avoided if all countries adopt a common international economic development plan that eradicates poverty and works to eliminate economic disparity throughout the world.

Creating a global economic development plan that frees all people to succeed on their own merits in any country discredits the propaganda of some tyrants that achieving prosperity is only possible for a limited number of elite.

A successful global effort to eradicate economic disparity will contradict the lie that violence, terrorism, and war are necessary to free the people from economic slavery created by the wealthier nations.

People are people, the same everywhere on every continent. Most people want the same things; peace, freedom and the opportunity to work and provide for their families. We all should respect each other seeking happiness and prosperity without imposing our will on others in the hope that we can achieve world peace for the first time once the severe poverty is eradicated.

WE KNOW NOW that protected private property rights and the right to borrow capital to invest in an appreciating asset, such as a home or business, empowers all people and permits them to raise their standard of living. This process, which has created prosperity in many countries, is applicable and viable in all countries no matter what level of education, societal, or environmental conditions exist currently.

WE KNOW NOW that people from other countries are no different from us. We share similar abilities and mindsets that seek a common prosperity.

WE KNOW NOW that we can no longer pretend that those living in economic slavery are not our concern. We are brothers and sisters on this little planet, with the same needs and desires. Most people do not seek power to manipulate others. Most are not corrupt. Most are not criminals. Most want peace and safety for their families.

WE KNOW NOW that there are billions of good people on this planet; individuals and families who desire a better life and are willing to work for it. Yet hundreds of millions cannot find employment. They search for food and find only crumbs. Each day they must think, "Am I of less value than those who live in luxury?"

WE KNOW NOW that adopting this economic development plan will eradicate poverty and increase global prosperity. Putting this plan to work refutes the devastating propaganda spread by leaders in many countries, that somehow people in more prosperous countries are to blame. Actually it is the leaders themselves who have purposely failed to establish economic freedom and opportunities for all of their own people.

WE KNOW NOW that regarding free trade as the sole method of raising the standard of living in underdeveloped countries is a myth. The true path to a higher standard of living becomes obvious when we understand and implement the principles of participatory economics. Participatory economics makes it plain that people with true freedom are the driving force for economic development and prosperity.

WE KNOW NOW, according to the published statistics of international organizations, that globalization in its many forms is failing the majority of people in underdeveloped countries. Poverty has increased in many countries and the disparity of income within and between countries has grown. A few people have become very wealthy while hundreds of millions working at low wage jobs are left out of the economic process that creates prosperity.

WE KNOW NOW that global economic development agencies have been unable to find a method of coping with universal poverty. Various aid programs and loans have caused major economic chaos in some countries when imposed without an understanding of the global economics involved. Some programs actually increased income disparity in emerging nations.

These misguided attempts to finance emerging economies enslaved people in minimum wage jobs that did not dramatically improve the economy. Nor did they provide them the opportunity to participate in economic growth as the countries became burdened with debt.

WE KNOW NOW that making loans to governments and corporations in developing countries, rather than lending money to the people, only creates lower wage job which are desperately needed. It does not provide an opportunity for the people to be free and prosperous. It is economic colonialism.

WE KNOW NOW why the principles of participatory economics are valid. Providing loans to people so they can invest in homes and businesses is an economic principle that reduces poverty by leveraging the labor and income of the people. When money borrowed to buy a home turns over in a country's economy year after year, it provides jobs in all industries and creates prosperity for all people.

WE KNOW NOW that the security and safety made possible by private property ownership is a natural right of the people. The first obligation of benevolent leaders who serve the people is to protect that right.

WE KNOW NOW that countries that recognize the natural right of the people to own property and businesses have experienced a rapid improvement in their standard of living.

WE **KNOW NOW** that home ownership is possible for all working people if home mortgages are insured and interest rates are lowered. Poverty can be eradicated when banks are structured to encourage all working people to buy a quality home, even those with minimum wage incomes.

WE KNOW NOW that International Mortgage Insurance has been the missing element in the effort to help struggling economies. International Mortgage Insurance makes major funding available for development by reducing the risk of mortgage lenders. Having global financial communities to fund home mortgages in emerging economies creates a critical economic incentive for governments to restructure their laws to establish and protect property rights. We are willing participants in helping to launch a global home building industry.

WE KNOW NOW that reducing economic disparity between and within countries provides hope that it is possible to avert an international economic depression and perhaps even a global war. Adding billions of people to the ranks of homeowners and product consumers must become an international priority. Industrializing more nations in order to hold down labor costs only increases global manufacturing capacity, without increasing product demand, while continuing to deprive people of the opportunity to prosper. Attempting to add additional manufacturing capacity without additional product consumers will increase the glut of products on the international market, leading to more financial problems for manufacturers and national economies.

WE KNOW NOW that the governments that are participatory democracies have the obligation to protect their people from aggressors and terrorists. They also have an equal obligation to protect the political and economic freedom of people everywhere. We must never forget that people are people…whether they live in Africa or Asia, North or South America, Europe or the Caribbean or the islands of the Pacific. We are the same.

WE KNOW NOW that there are approximately four billion men, women, and children, and three billion yet to be born over the next forty years, destined to live in abject poverty because there are those that seek to control their nation's economy for their personal purposes and refuse to guarantee private property rights for the people.

WE KNOW NOW how to create jobs in the 21ˢᵗ century that will develop prosperous economies and eradicate poverty, wherever true economic freedom exists. This process can lead to global peace as international friction due to economic disparity is reduced. People will have a reasonable expectation that they can be prosperous as long as we are at peace.

WE KNOW NOW there are no more excuses for our failure. If we are to be a humane people we must act to bring about prosperity for all and a hope for peace. If any of us fail to act in support of this plan now that we know there is a solution, we become co-conspirators with those who will choose to ignore this proposal and continue to hold their people in economic slavery.

FIRST
ADDENDUM

The genesis for this approach to the eradication of global poverty came from the passage below that was written over two hundred years ago.

Declaration of Independence,

We hold these Truths to be self-evident, that all Men are created equal, that they are endowed by their Creator with certain inalienable Rights that among these are Life, Liberty, and the Pursuit of Happiness. That to secure these Rights, Governments are instituted among Men, deriving their just Powers from the Consent of the Governed, that whenever any Form of Government becomes destructive of these Ends, it is the Right of the People to alter or to abolish it, and to institute a new Government, laying its Foundation on such Principles, and organizing its Powers in such Form, as to them shall seem most likely to affect their Safety and Happiness.

Prudence, indeed, will dictate that Governments long established should not be changed for light and transient Causes; and accordingly all Experience hath shewn, that Mankind are more disposed to suffer, while Evils are sufferable, than to right themselves by abolishing the Forms to which they are accustomed. But when a long Train of Abuses and Usurpations, pursuing invariably the same object, evinces a Design to reduce them under absolute Despotism, it is their Right, it is their Duty, to throw off such a Government, and to provide new Guards for their future Security.

SECOND
ADDENDUM

TWELVE ECONOMIC PRINCIPLES THAT CREATE PROSPEROUS PEOPLE AND NATIONS

These principles are discussed in Chapter Four and are included here for your quick reference, copying, and transmittal.

1. Private Property Rights Enable the People to Invest in The Economy

Establishment of private property rights for individuals and businesses is the first principle of the natural law of economics that must govern the sovereignty over any nation attempting to create an environment in which all people are able to work and become prosperous. Providing a clear and unequivocal right under the constitution of a nation for the people to own private property creates prosperity because the people are enabled to own an appreciating asset. Any nation whose constitution does not provide for laws granting private property rights to the people prevents them from becoming prosperous by purchasing an appreciating asset and being able to finance the acquisition through mortgage financing utilizing the ownership of the asset as collateral.

2. Judicial Rectitude Protects Private Property Rights.

It is absolutely critical that private property rights be protected by the establishment and enforcement of a constitutional right guaranteeing such as well as the validity of legal contracts of title under the rule of the law. This also reduces the burden on judicial authorities in determining the rightful ownership and legal liens in the event of disputes.

Reliance on the legal process both domestically and internationally is essential for the protection of lenders when extending credit to prospective homeowners and for the homeowner when entering into contracts.

3. Only The Credit Worthy Borrowers Become The Homebuyers.

The key financing principle that establishes the feasibility for making home loans in emerging economies is the loaning of money initially to people who qualify for a loan to purchase a quality, modern home. These borrowers have established income records that show their ability to pay the mortgage payments. This reduces the risks to lenders and the number of defaults on home loans. Reducing risks increases the number of financial institutions willing to invest in home mortgages in emerging economies. The credit worthiness of the people determines the strength of the economy of any nation where homebuilding is the predominate industry that creates jobs.

4. Construction of Quality Housing Creates – The Moving Up Effect.

The purchase of new homes by the employed and the affluent creates vacancies when they move into their new home. This creates an opportunity for others to move up into better homes and apartments vacated by those who have moved into a new home. Those moving up also leave behind vacancies that become opportunities for others to move up and the cycle repeats itself. It is important to understand this phenomenon when attempting to provide homes for the homeless. The annual number of homebuyers moving up by selling one existing home and purchasing another averages three times the number of initial new homebuyers in the United States. For every million new homes constructed, three million additional homeowners are able to move up into a better home.

This will be true of any nation once the process begins to build homes and there is an increase in employment and wages. Building quality homes for those that qualify for a loan is a process that increases the number of quality homes in every city, eliminating the need to construct "affordable" housing of little value and limited life that do not appreciate in value over time.

The homes that are vacated at the bottom of the price range are older homes that have been vacated because the owner qualified for a home of better quality. However, it is important to recognize that most of the older homes were well constructed in their time. They undoubtedly need maintenance and repairs and a thorough cleaning and painting. Because the homes are of a standard size and sound construction, there will be an increase in value as the mortgage is paid off. When selling a home to the newly employed and first time qualifier, it is mandatory that the home being sold to the first homebuyer is an asset that has an inherent value that will appreciate. If this is not possible, the first homebuyer is in effect "still paying rent" on a home that will not increase his net worth and will eventually be torn down.

5. Owning an Appreciating Asset Increases Net Worth.

A national law that protects the natural right of people to borrow the necessary funds to leverage their income and purchase an appreciating asset such as a home is the key to creating prosperity for all people.

The home appreciates and increases in value over time as the former rent payments become the source of funds being spent, sometimes by more than one family, to reduce the principal of the debt increasing the net worth of the homeowner. It is in essence a forced savings program that is secured by a tangible asset and increases the owner's sense of security.

The most important characteristic of the process is that the money being borrowed from a bank is only for the specific purpose of buying an appreciating asset. The borrowed funds are based on appraisals and spent only for acquiring products and services needed for the construction of a modern home and a share of public services. A specific loan amount funded by local banks based on appraisals eliminates the corruption that is sometimes associated with investing in emerging economies.

Money spent by governments, corporations, or by the people for any other types of products or services will not increase the net worth of the people. Increasing their net worth is the essential requirement for the economy of any nation to become prosperous. It is the willingness of those with jobs to take risks and use their credit to acquire an appreciating asset or business that energizes every successful economy.

6. Insured Mortgages Increases the Number of Qualifying Borrowers.

Providing mortgage insurance for home loans is the key to achieving the greatest success in building homes for all who qualify in developing economies. Mortgage insurance dramatically increases the number of potential lower income buyers that can qualify. It lowers the interest rate on the loan to the lowest achievable rate.

Lowering the interest rate is critical for this plan to be successful because the lower income group that will then be able to qualify is the largest and has the greatest need. By this procedure, international and domestic financial institutions are protected when extending credit in emerging economies. Foreign lenders investing in a subsidiary or domestically owned banks in developing economies can rely on the loan being backed by specific loan values based on appraisals and mortgage insurance provided by the domestic banks in the local economy.

7. Guaranteed Title Establishes Legal Ownership.

The establishment, public acknowledgement, and recording of the legal descriptions for private property are a fundamental requirement for private property ownership and transfer of land. In some countries, this will require the establishment of legal descriptions for the land for the first time. This is now a very practical and precise engineering process made possible by the various Global Positioning Systems (GPS) that are currently available. Once any specific point is selected as the base line measurements of property, boundaries can be taken utilizing standard engineering procedures and checked by additional GPS readings. In the event land formerly held by a government or large tract owner is sold for the development of homes and communities, the seller must provide proof of ownership, the description of the land and the right to the lender financing the home mortgage.

8. Quality Construction Creates Educated and Trained Workers

The construction of the millions of homes for the employed, whether they are teachers, policemen, government workers, or any affluent group, increases the number of people that must be educated and trained on the job. Education and training in the real estate disciplines, including construction, engineering, and legal title, escrows, designs, appraisals, financing, and banking, are key to the eradication of poverty. Education coupled with the creation of jobs is the strength of this plan. Developers constructing homes will also be able to invite members of other countries to participate in the training and they will take the education and experience home for the management of their own program.

9. Newly Employed Become Qualified Buyers.

The newly employed that are being trained on the job in real estate disciplines become qualified for buying one of the homes vacated by others moving up. Building new homes for the newly employed increases the number of homes constructed. This increase in employment also expands the aggregate demand for all types of consumer services and products domestically and globally as their income is spent and passes through the hands of other people. Borrowing money and repaying over 30 years energizes an economy and begins the process of creating prosperity. The home loans are actually financing the increase in manufacturing through the creation of demand for consumer products.

The international investment community must establish new rules and requirements for all new buyers. The sale of mortgage backed bonds is anticipated to be worldwide. Domestic investors must require lending standards that can be agreed upon internationally to insure worldwide sale and distribution of the mortgages.

10. Demand for Consumer Products Increases Domestic & Global Employment.

The increase in employment in the home building industry provides income for the newly employed in all sectors of the economy, enabling them to increase the aggregate demand for consumer products that increases manufacturing employment. As the capital expended for the land, construction of the building, acquisition of equipment and labor is released into the economy of a developing nation, it passes through the hands of the people. As they spend, the funds turn over and over, creating a demand for consumer products and services many times greater than the original cost of the home even after paying taxes on each turn over. Over time, the manufactures in emerging economies will have to expand. New companies must be formed to provide for the refrigerators, heaters, air conditioners, furniture, and clothing needed in addition to the construction materials. The home loans are actually funding the expansion of the global manufacturing capacity through the creation of consumer demand.

As the economy begins to expand, the demand for skilled and educated people to work in all sectors of the economy will increase in other countries as well.

A housing industry creates demand for products and services, many of which will not be initially available domestically and have to be imported. This impacts the economies of other nations. The demand created by initially expending billions of dollars annually in a home building industry will succeed in creating prosperity and energizing the global economy where aid and loans to governments in the past has consistently failed. Empirical evidence shows that when housing construction is booming in the United States, imports also increase. When housing construction slows in the U.S. the economies of other countries are impacted.

11. Home Equity Collateral - Small Business Loans.

The increased value of the home equity, the money invested in an appreciating asset such as a home or a parcel of land, over time becomes the predominate source of collateral for personal loans. The homeowner's equity in a personal asset makes it possible to borrow funds for financing the operation of privately owned small businesses. Small businesses are the principal employers in prosperous countries when the economy is based on protected private property rights. In countries where protected private property rights exist, well over 66% of the employed work for small businesses. Home equity loans are the critical component for increasing the number of small businesses. They are the driving force when attempting to increase employment in every national economy where the people are truly prosperous.

12. Taxes On Proceeds From Home Loans Used For City Wide Infrastructure and Services.

Taxing the home building industry strengthens the viability of governments and enables the repayment of loans borrowed for the construction of infrastructure, medical facilities, and schools as well as and supporting the needs of the people throughout all sections of a city.

A tax increase also provides capital for the repayment of loans used for construction of facilities for services and infrastructure needed for the specific home building community such as streets, waste and water treatment. The home building process also includes fees to be paid to governments on the construction of each new home. This will fund the new homeowner's share of the cost to extend and provide utilities and roads to each home.

In fact, a mathematical analysis of the various forms of taxation which includes all sales tax, income tax, and government fees charged at every level, will show the governments will receive almost 100% of the mortgage funds expended for development and construction. Depending on the tax rate it occurs in over a period of eight to ten years as the home loan proceeds move through the economy and sales and income are taxed at each turn over.

THIRD
ADDENDUM
WHAT YOU CAN DO

INTERNATIONAL PROSPERITY
NETWORK

Billions of people are waiting. Can you continue to ignore them? You know how to eradicate poverty. You know that the financial capacity exists to help them. Is it possible for you to remain indifferent now and still believe we are a civilized planet? Are you willing to join an INTERNATIONAL PROSPERITY NETWORK (IPN) to created jobs and eradicated poverty?

CREATING JOBS IN THE 21ST CENTURY has four goals that are the guidelines of IPN.

1. AWARENESS: The first purpose is to raise worldwide awareness to the fact that there is a new economic development paradigm that is viable for creating jobs and eradicating poverty in countries needing assistance. It is the first step of an the International Prosperity Network effort to reduce the necessity for immigration by creating jobs that will eradicate poverty and create global prosperity, which will reduce economic disparity, improve trade, and encourage peace between nations.

2. EDUCATION: The second purpose of the book is to provide an educational tool for you to use in the spreading the message of hope to people in your country. Talk to others that you may know in other countries that are concerned about severe poverty or unemployment. Teach people how the plan creates prosperity. Utilize the internet for

more information about this book and its associated blogs if you have access to an online computer. Refer people to the web site, **www. buildglobal.org**, for more information about the activities of those who are becoming active. Sign up with comments and suggestions and indicate your willingness to be contacted by others. Teach them that there is a viable and practical solution to the problem of global unemployment and poverty. Share this plan with others of like humanitarian interests. Purchase more copies of this book on-line and send gift copies to those who are leaders within your country. Sign up on the web site, to receive updates on what is happening. You can start your own Face Book or blog and engage people in the education process online using our existing blogs.

3. INTERNATIONAL VOCABULARY: The third purpose is to provide a common international vocabulary and outline of the many elements that make up the process for financing and constructing homes. It is a process of bringing people together and making action plans in each participating country. With the publication of this book, the author intends to form a non-profit foundation in the United States to provide guidance and funding for men and women worldwide whose goal is the total and complete eradication of severe poverty.

4. ESTABLISH AN EXAMPLE: To encourage emerging economies to accelerated their efforts to create jobs and eradicate poverty as Mexico is doing. The examples will illustrate that the funding of home construction not only increases the prosperity of the home owner, and the newly employed, the taxation of the process provides the means for the nation to pay for the infrastructure improvements needed to support the increase in prosperous activity without incurring debt.

The following are suggested tasks for you that may wish to become involved.
- Organize and seek out those that would share your goals, understand the plan, and are willing to step out and lead.

Organize personal discussions and informal meetings as well as more formal organizations in cities worldwide. Discuss and interact with those willing to take these steps together to create the reality.

• Work to prepare the laws that will encourage international financing of homes in your country. Forward data collected to the blogs for others to read.

• Organize trusts, non-profit foundations, and companies that can raise funds to support candidates seeking to gain office and become active in supporting the home building effort. Develop and attract corporations and lenders interested in own specific programs that will lead to constructing homes.

These efforts are to seek to teach and help others to understand what is needed to establish the development paradigm.

• Your country of origin or current residence does not matter. The program is designed to use the internet and other electronic means to spread the word to all nations.

• Media must become active participants in a global community effort to raise awareness.

• This paradigm for increasing employment and creating prosperity must be adopted if there is to be any hope for reducing economic disparity and achieving peace.

• Foundations dedicated to assisting the poor throughout the world must be given the opportunity to identify the role they would like to play as part of a global organization in the eradicating of severe poverty.

- Financial institutions must be given the opportunity to join this global movement. Global financial interest will determine which countries have domestic banks interested securing international financing for the purpose of home building.

- They can work with domestic banks in participating countries to finance mortgages for home loans. The interest of the international financial community will provide momentum to those planning a home building program for their country.

- Business leaders in countries that are receptive to the principles of economic freedom in their country must step forward and insure that there are protected, private, property rights for all people.

- Men and women everywhere must be sought out to assist in the passage of new constitutional laws if necessary to establish private property rights

- Legal descriptions must be established based on a GPS mapping of land ownership that is needed as security for loans in each country.

- Schools must be established to teach the disciplines of real estate development, financing and construction. Many of the instructors will be returning to their native countries with skills learned as immigrants in the more industrialized countries.

- Men and women in all countries must be recruited to organize pro-active groups and foundations for the encouragement of governments and corporations to work together to establish agreements and legal guidelines for lending on homes internationally.

- Title management companies must be invited to take part in the establishment of title companies. Legal descriptions for countries without basic survey information must be instituted. Real estate finance companies around the world will be invited to be a part of the discussion with leaders in perspective countries and financial institutions to encourage the adoption of participating economics.

- Global real estate development companies must be encouraged to help emerging companies in each of the countries planning to organize and develop housing projects.

- Global construction companies must be encouraged to take the initiative to help existing domestic companies in the participating countries in planning, design, and construction to the International Standard using the most current engineering principles.

The refinement of these actions and many more yet to be identified will lead to an international movement on many fronts for the eradication of severe poverty and the creation of jobs in the 21st century. Once this new economic development paradigm is understood people will believe the time has come. The problems of organizing an international effort to economically free four billion people that are suffering from hunger, homelessness, and the lack of medical care can be resolved. We now know that it can be done if we are serious about helping those in need.

GLOSSARY
A GLOBAL VOCABULARY

This glossary is provided for those readers who are unfamiliar with the terms used for real estate development and construction in United States. These are the same processes and concepts that will be used when developing real estate and constructing home in the emerging countries.

Aggregate Demand: It is the total of all expenditures on goods and services of any national or state economy. Expenditures include all forms of investments, goods purchased for consumption, and government expenditures added to the total value of all exports, less value of all imports.

Asset: It is an item that can be possessed and has useful attributes. It is tangible and can be sold or exchanged for something else of value. The ownership of an asset such as a home or a commercial building that house industrial, retail,, or offices normally increases in wealth over time. Real property assets, such as land, buildings, crops, or mineral rights increase more rapidly in value during times of inflation.

Amortization: The act of repayment of a loan, sometimes referred to as extinguishing or liquidating a debt (reducing the principal owed) such as a mortgage, normally by paying monthly payments (called installments) of interest and principal over a specified period such as thirty years. Principal payments are graduated and increase over time as the interest on the declining balance becomes less in a manner that holds the monthly payment constant.

Bond: A legal document that certifies that the owner has the legal right to receive a specified portion of the payments on a debt being extinguished by payments to the company or government that issued the loan. Terms of repayment specify the number of years (term) the loan will be outstanding and the number of payment associated with the interest rate or yield rate until the principal has been paid in full.

Bonds, Tax-Free: The buyer of tax-free bond is not required to pay income taxes on the interest received from the purchase of the bond by national or local laws in the country where the tax-free bonds are sold to the public. Tax free bonds are sold at a lower interest rate because the buyer is willing to receive a lower interest return since he does not have to pay income taxes. Because the bonds are tax-free, the mortgages issued for the financing of the homes have a lower interest rate for the borrower than would normally be expected. In effect, tax free bonds lower the interest cost to the homeowner as well as help to increase their net worth.

Brain Drain: The immigration of educated and/or experienced workers by whatever means, legal and illegal, from underdeveloped to foreign countries in search of work in order to survive and support family members left behind.

Free Market: A marketplace, either local or international where there is commerce free of government interference or regulation. This creates one of the conditions for true economic freedom when the supply and demand sectors of the economy operate without restriction.

Free Trade: This is a term that is normally used to describe national policies of non-intervention by governments in regard to trade between countries, such as not imposing tariffs on less expensive goods entering the country.

This theoretical concept that is not practiced, suggests that this type of trade would increase global prosperity. There must be major reduction in the disparity between nations before this theory has a chance of becoming a reality. This is one of the goals of Build Global; the new economic development paradigm proposed.

Fredrick von Hayek Economics: Hayek advanced the economic principle that people working to acquire capital and spending it to create demand for consumer products is the only method by which an economy can become prosperous.

Gross Domestic Product: The total of all goods and services for a period of one year generated and sold in the national economy plus the cost of goods exported, less the cost of imports.

Gross Domestic Product per Capita: It is the Gross Domestic Product divided by the population of the nation.

Home Insurance: A company issues a policy or legal document agreeing to assume the risk for paying a portion of the buyer's risk of owning a home. It pays to the buyer money for a portion or all of a loss experienced by the buyer from a fire or acts of nature.

Inflation: A rise in the cost of goods purchased, or increases in prices generally measured over a specified period of time in comparison to a predetermined base price. This can be caused by an increase in demand for products that exceed the ability of the market to supply in a timely manner due to sudden increase in the supply of money available to the purchasers.

Interest: The amount of money owed annually for use of money borrowed, expressed as a percent of the amount borrowed. Interest is paid monthly in addition to a portion of the principal necessary to reduce the amount of debt or principal owned.

Keynesian Economics: The economist Johns Maynard Keyes believed that the economy of a country could become prosperous by increasing aggregate demand through the intervention of the government in the economy by increasing government spending, increasing taxes, and borrowing and creating debt.

Mortgage: A legal document which conveys a right of ownership of an asset to another party, a lender, in turn for loaning money on the asset owned by the borrower in the event of default on payments. The asset acts as security, for the promise to repay the debt. Security means the lender is given the right to take possession of the asset in the event the borrower fails to meet the terms of repayment.

Home Mortgage Insurance: A company known as an insurance agency agrees to pay to a lender (bank) the amount of any loss suffered by the bank on each loan made by the lender to a homebuyer, in the event the lender must foreclose on the loan by taking possession of the home because of insufficient payments. The amount paid by the insurance agency is normally only that amount of loss the lender experiences after taking possession, sells the home and receives less than owed on the mortgage. The insurance agency charges a fee for each loan dependent on the evaluation of the credit of the general population borrowing funds for the purchase of a home or building. The establishment of Home Mortgage Insurance reduces the risk to the lender and lowers the rate of interest, thereby increasing the number of potential borrowers that can qualify for a mortgage because the monthly payment is reduced.

Mortgage-backed Bonds: These are bonds backed by mortgage loans originated by the banks. The purchase of the mortgage-backed bonds includes the right for the buyer to hold the mortgages and receive the payments made by the homeowner.

They may also sell a collection or pool of mortgages to the public on a stock market in the form of bonds secured by the income from the mortgages. The money paid by the buyer of the bond is used by the lenders to originate more mortgages.

Participatory Democracy: This term is defined for the purposes of this book to include both the direct voting process and the process of electing representatives. This emphasizes that the people who can exercise this right control the government by either method and are not managed by some form of dictatorial government. Under participatory democracy people are able to establish laws permitting the populace to enjoy the benefits of participatory economics.

Participatory Economics: This principle, as defined for the purposes of this book, is the right to participate as borrowers and investors in the economy of a nation by having the protected right to own property, homes and businesses. This is the basis of creating jobs and demand for consumer products which creates prosperity.

Pass-through Securities: These are legal instruments showing that the owner of the security holds an undivided ownership interest in a collection or pool of mortgages on which homeowners are making payment. The purchaser of the security, normally sold in the form of a bond, is entitled to receive a specified portion of the monthly payments of principal and interest made by the homeowner on the mortgage as the funds are passed through.

Principal (Loan Principal): Refers to the amount of the debt incurred when borrowing money.

Private Property: Assets such as land or a home belonging to a specific person or a family are identified as private property. It is referred to as private property if the owner has the sole right to determine its development and disposition without interference, except to be subject to local planning.

Private Property Rights: These are rights guaranteed and protected by the government that support the principles of Economic Freedom. They are related to the ownership and use of goods and services, stock in companies, and assets such as land or homes, buildings, and personal property. The rights permit the owner to use and modify the asset, to borrow money on the asset, and to sell the asset independently without approval of any government. The property cannot be taken by a government without just compensation and then only for the purpose of the common good.

Property Lien: In the event of default on a loan the lender has the legal right to take possession of the asset and sell the asset to a third party as a means of recovering the money loaned. Upon borrowing the money, the public is normally put on notice that the asset cannot be sold by the borrower without the repayment of the debt or without the approval of the lender. This is referred to as having a lien on the property or the right to hold or take possession and sell, applying the proceeds toward the repayment of the loan. Upon repayment of the loan, the right to take possession of the asset, the lien is removed.

BIBLIOGRAPHY

[1] Bernard Baumohl, <u>The Secrets of Economic Indicators</u> (New Jersey, Wharton School of Publishing, 2005)

[2] Friedrich August Hayek, <u>The Road to Serfdom</u>, (Chicago, Ill, The University of Chicago Press. 1944, Renewed 1972)

[3] Dick Morris & Eileen McGann, <u>Catastrophe ...And How To Fight Back</u>, (United States of America, HarperCollins. 2009)

[4] John Maynard Keynes, <u>The General Theory of Employment, Interest, and Money</u>, (United Kingdom, Palgrave Macmillan. 1936)

[5] Michel Chossudovsky and Andrew Gavin Marshall, Editors The <u>Global Economic Crisis, (Montreal, Quebec,</u> Global Research Publishers. 2010)

[6] Laurie Garrett, <u>Betrayal of Trust, The Collapse of Global Public Health,</u> (New York, Hyperion 2000)

[7] Hernando De Soto, <u>the Mystery of Capital, Why Capitalism Triumphs In The West and Fails Everywhere Else</u> (New York, Basic Books 2009)

[8] Ambassador Mark Palmer, <u>Breaking the Real Axis of Evil, How To Oust the World's Last Dictators by 2005</u> (Lanham, Maryland: Rowman & Littlefield Publishers, Inc. 2003)

[9] Tom Bethell, <u>The Noblest Triumph, Property and Prosperity Through The Ages</u>, (New York, Sr. Martin's Press, 1998)

[10] Daniel Yergin and Joseph Stanislaw, <u>The Commanding Heights, The Battle Between Government and The Market Place That is Remaking The Modern World</u>, (New York, SIMON & SCHUSTER, 1998)

[11] Bernard Baumohl, <u>The Secrets of Economic Indicators</u> (New Jersey, Wharton School of Publishing, 2005) (Quoted on pg. 144)

[12] Joseph Stiglitz, <u>Fair Trade For All</u> (Oxford University Press 2005)

www.ingramcontent.com/pod-product-compliance
Lightning Source LLC
Chambersburg PA
CBHW051448170526
45166CB00001B/161